AFTER THE RAILWAY

One Man's Journey Through World War and Civil Conflict at the end of Empire

Roland Crooke

AFTER THE RAILWAY:

Life, Death And Family In South East Asia

A Memoir of the End of Empire

The Crooke family

FOREWORD

My father, John Crooke, grew up in Berkhamsted in Hertfordshire, between the two world wars. Joining the Army at the start of the Second World War, he was part of the humiliating surrender at Singapore in 1942, and endured nearly four years in terrible captivity, including a year as slave labour on the "Death Railway" in Thailand. He returned to Malaya in 1947 to manage a rubber estate and brought up a family there during a civil war or liberation struggle, depending on your viewpoint. His humility, gentleness and compassion won him many friends amongst the "colonised" as well as the "colonisers", and we will follow him and his family through the momentous events which formed the backdrop to his life, until his departure from Malaya in 1969 and his death in 1987.

The book starts with a picture of his daily life as a rubber planter in the 1950s before returning to his childhood, and following him through the Second World War, terrible captivity in the jungles of Thailand and his later return to live and work in the same South East Asian landscape.

We will look at the everyday human relations between some ordinary people in this version of the imperial project, and the impact they have had on each other until the present day. John's story will remind us of the oh so human, grey areas in Britain's imperial history, all too often written in black and white. Within the structure developed by the colonisers, I want to show how ordinary people on both sides of the power relationship negotiated close and affectionate relationships.

This book is intended to honour my father but may also serve as an alternative to more academic, sometimes ideological approaches to recording the British Empire. These have tended to portray it as either unalloyed evil, or as a nostalgic refuge from the harsh realities of the modern world. My hope is that this small story stands as an account of how human beings can survive bitter tribulations to make strong connections across culture.

Thanks go to many who have encouraged and supported my effort to tell a story about the end of Empire. Its genesis was a memoir about John Crooke's war experiences ("An Ordinary Man") which tracked his progress up and back down the Siam Burma Railway between 1942 and 1945, which I completed in 2009. One or two misguided individuals over the next few years have thought it deserved some amplification and a wider audience.

More recently, Dr Laura Carter, of the University of Paris, who specialises in British post-war social history, thought that the story warranted expansion to cover the post-war period and the end of empire, taking in the perspective of both colonisers and colonised. Grateful thanks to her and others who have offered support and advice, now including Clem Flanagan, my editor at Cornerstones Agency.

Most people in this story retain their own names, but I have decided to change the names of the members of my extended family in Malaysia. I am grateful to "Ravi", who has helped greatly to ensure accuracy in events relevant to him and his family.

In the end, though, in this as in so much else I owe most to Helen Crooke. From the moment I met her, she has "got" my connection with Malaysia and encouraged me to nurture it. To be prepared to fly halfway across the world with a three-year-old child and three-month-old baby to meet me after a four-week absence is an indication of her quality. One of my few regrets is that John never met her. I think they would have liked each other.

Roland Crooke
December 2020

This is for you Pa.

CONTENTS

CHAPTER 1

Dawn, August 15, 1955
Emergency State Black

A battered Austin Gypsy jeep stands outside a rambling, black and white painted wooden bungalow on top of a hill. The hill overlooks a thousand acres of newly planted rubber trees, bordering several thousand more mature trees stretching into the distance. This is Sungei Toh Pawang, a British owned rubber estate in the northern Malayan state of Kedah.

Fig 1: The 'first' house pictured in 1993. No longer black and white, but still partly a home.

The sun rises, as it always does at this spot near the equator, at 6.30 am. Cockerels crow and local "pi" dogs unfold and scratch themselves before ambling off to forage. Soon the full force of Malaya's heat and humidity will stun everything and everybody into submission, but for now all is cool. In the kitchen to the side of the house, Ramu, the cook, has made early morning tea and is starting breakfast. The smell and then sound of burnt toast being scraped can be heard. Roland will grow up convinced that this scraping is an integral part of the toast making process. The rest of the house is quiet; Devi, the amah, is preparing the downstairs area for its morning purpose as a nursery school for local children.

From some corrugated iron huts at the back of the house emerges a lanky, dark skinned South Indian man in white shirt and khaki trousers. He is the jeep's driver, named Veloo. From the other side of the house amble two shorter, Malay men dressed in jungle green fatigues and bush hats, cradling Lee Enfield jungle carbines in their arms. They are Special Constables, auxiliary policemen whose task is to protect the Estate's manager and three assistant managers. The SCs have been recruited to keep watch overnight on the white planters and their families (though John suspects that they do not always stay awake) and act as bodyguards during the day which has now started. They are rural members of the Malay community in Malaya, which provides, almost exclusively, the membership of the police forces combatting the largely Chinese Malayan Races Liberation Army (MRLA).

Fig 2: John with SC personal protection detail - not at all asleep!

The three meet up near the jeep and exchange polite, but reserved greetings. These three men have worked together for some months, but as members of different races maintain a discreet distance from each other. Moments later, they're joined from the front of the house by a slightly built 35-year-old white man, of medium height, dressed in long khaki shorts and a short-sleeved flannel shirt. A holstered revolver is strapped to his right hip and he is carrying a Lee Enfield jungle carbine. He has receding dark hair, a prominent nose, and a cheerful smile. He returns the rather lackadaisical salutes from the three other men. The man is accompanied by a small, excitable Scottish Terrier dog which he encourages to jump nimbly into the well of the front passenger seat before getting in himself. Veloo and the SCs get into the driver's and rear passenger seats, giving a wide berth to the dog. The white man checks the carbine's safety catch and places it within reach on the dashboard of the jeep. The SCs slip the safety catches off their weapons

The white man has worked on Sungei Toh Pawang Rubber Estate for the last 8 years and is about to start his morning round of the estate. Partly this is about ensuring that the labourers are all properly tasked to cut lalang, the sharp local grass, tap trees, collect latex- the rubber tree sap which will when processed become rubber- or carry out other jobs keeping the estate productive. But it's also about making sure he is visible to the workforce, not hiding away behind the armour-plated sheets fixed to the inside walls of his bungalow, or in his office elsewhere on the estate. He can see and be seen, take the temperature of the workforce and pick-up unhappiness or fears early. Although this is a relatively safe area, the Emergency, as the Malayan civil unrest is euphemistically known, has been in progress for eight years and "Communist Terrorists" have recently held up a trailer load of workers on the estate, ditched their latex and read them a lecture on the evils of imperialism. On other estates, supervisors have been shot as an example. What he knows as he starts his day is that there is little support among his workers for the "CTs", but a lot of understandable fear that they will become targets for them. The workforce is mostly first- or second-generation indentured Tamil migrants from Southern India.

This is his favourite time of day, touring his part of the estate, which stretches to more than 5000 acres, and talking to the workers as the sun begins its climb...

In a mixture of Tamil and Malay, the driver and manager greet each other and plan the day:

"Peace on your morning, uncle."

"And on yours, Tuan. Division one today?"

"Yes, the far end. I want to see the people the Bintang Tiga held up yesterday."

All rubber estates work to a similar rhythm. The trees stand in serried ranks, and are tapped in rotation, using a chisel like hand tool which scrapes off the scab of solidified latex left in a spiral pattern from the last tapping, and allows new latex to flow round and down the tree's trunk to a pottery cup in a metal bracket. Tapping is always done early in the morning because the latex is flowing most strongly then. Each tapper has a daily task comprising a parcel of trees which must first be tapped and then the latex collected in one of two former kerosene tins suspended from a pole carried across the shoulders. The rotation system means that the tappers are moved out to different bits of the estate in tractor towed trailers each day; some of them quite remote.

Fig 3: Bringing the latex in

It is in one of these remoter spots that a band of MRLA guerrillas/CTs appeared the day before. By mid-1955, "bandit" activity in Kedah has reduced to the point where many parts of the state are designated "white" or clear of MRLA activity. Sungei Toh Pawang is not one of them currently, but even here, MRLA cadres, nicknamed Bintang Tiga, or Three Stars, after the motif on the caps they wore, are under pressure.

The "New Village" system, under which Chinese villagers must live in enclosed, guarded communities, has to a great extent cut the guerrillas off from their main source of support and supply. The half dozen or so fighters who have emerged from the jungle are poorly armed and equipped, half-starved and ill with malaria, desperately interested in any food and medicine the workers are carrying.

They line all the terrified labourers tasked to tap the rubber trees up at gun point together with their Kangany. Once they have the slim pickings in food and drink they collect from them, they lecture the workers but do not kill any of them or their equally terrified fore-man. Instead, they read them a long lecture from their own clandes-tine newspaper. Then they burn the tractor and trailer and throw the tapped latex away. Who knows why these fighters behave with this odd sort of restraint? By this time in the conflict ordinary workers are generally spared not murdered - that fate is usually reserved for the supervisors, who are deemed to be collaborators. Maybe by this time, the "bandits" can see the writing on the wall and are them-selves looking for a way out. Any fighter turning themselves in to the British authorities would be interrogated and resettled but not punished. Instead, they get a cash payment depending on the value of the weapon they brought with them. A Bren light machine gun is lit-erally worth its weight in gold, whereas a machete style parang knife is worth only a few dollars. The same payment is made to anybody else bringing the weapon in, resulting in a steady trickle of fighters turning themselves in with the weapon of one of their comrades who had met an untimely end.

Fig 4: The Bintang Tiga send a message

Nevertheless, the incident would have been highly traumatic to the workers involved, and on this day the young manager understands that they need to see that life has returned to normality. This would be achieved partly by his visiting the work party which had been held up, but also by the rapid arrival the previous day of a quick reaction force of Gurkhas, the Nepalese mercenaries who had been part of the British Army since the mid-19th C. Their training depot is a few miles from the estate and their arrival in force reassures the workers (Appendix 1). They are accompanied by Iban trackers from Sarawak, formerly the private fiefdom of Raja Brooke in Borneo, who cast about for clues as to where the rag-tag band of fighters might have gone. Intelligence is now so plentiful that the security forces will probably know the identity of each of the fighters.

So, on this day, the tapped latex would be collected in the late morning by tractor towed tankers, before it had solidified, and taken to the estate factory for processing into sheets of crepe rubber. This would then be sent to the US and Europe for further processing.

The young white man is John Crooke. His unexceptional appearance belies a truly exceptional early life; one that has led him to this place today. Ten years ago, he and thousands of other prisoners of war were liberated from camps along the newly constructed Siam-Burma railway, probably shortly before they were due to be executed by their Japanese and Korean guards. Their lives were almost certainly saved by the detonation of atomic bombs over Hiroshima and Nagasaki, which brought about the deaths of thousands of Japanese and the surrender of Japan. By the time he was liberated by American and British special forces, John weighed almost exactly half what he weighed at the start of his captivity. He had survived starvation, cholera, and regular beatings from his guards. Now, a decade later, he has chosen to live and work just a few hundred miles from the scene of his wartime trauma.

Back at the black and white house Devi is opening the downstairs shutters and doors. This lets into the house the still cool breeze, smells, and noises.

Devi is married to Veloo, the lanky driver, and has worked for the Crookes since 1949, a year after Mary Crooke arrived to be with her husband. She will become an indispensable part of the household, and an Amah to Mary and John's two young children, Roland, and Celia. She and her family (Veloo, sons Pany and Ravi, daughters, Santha and Vasantha) live in quarters at the back of the Crooke house.

Fig 5: Playing in the garden (l to r Celia, Ravi, Devi and Roland)

What combination of circumstances makes Devi turn up at the Crookes' house that day in 1949 and tell (not ask) Mary that she is taking over running the house as *Amah*, is unclear.

Devi is small of stature with a mystical dignity I can still remember. As the mother of what finally became a family of two boys and two girls, her earning power was limited. The job of *Amah* in a European household would have come with free accommodation and food if she got on with the cook. If she could get her husband, Veloo, a job as John's driver that would be even better.

But I believe that Devi was motivated also by fellow feeling for another woman in trouble, understanding what Mary was going through in trying to set up a household in an alien place. Devi's attraction to Mary would have been the product of a complex bundle of economic and emotional impulses, that in a later time might come to be known as "Sisterhood".

And Mary never forgot what Devi had done for her. Much later, in a taped interview she gave to two of her grandchildren a few years before she died, she said "People thought of them as servants, but they weren't, they were friends."

Is this how that first conversation in 1949 went?

"Peace on your morning, Mem."

"Peace on your morning...Devi, is it? Ramu said you had an urgent message for me. What do you want?"

"Mem, I think you need some help with your house and your children. This is a strange country to you, but I understand it, and can look after you and your family. My family and I will live here (indicating the quarters at the back of the house) and do everything necessary to keep the house clean and your children safe. If Tuan wants, my husband can drive for him."

"Well, alright. One month's notice, and 100 dollars a month."

Reflection: *It seems likely that Mary would have incurred much disapproval from the expat community for this unorthodox way of employing staff and deserves congratulation for that reason alone. But however it happened, Devi and her family coming to live with John's family changed everybody's lives. Until the age of 6 I had an extended family of three sisters and two brothers, and two mothers. We will see how, as the pull of boarding school and England* *became more powerful as Celia and I grew older, this strong frame-work became gradually weakened, to my huge regret.*

CHAPTER 2

A Different World

John is reading a Biggles story in his favourite chair in Aunt Phyllis's little cottage. Elsewhere he can hear Hugh and Pat having a noisy quarrel over her old wooden train set. The three brothers have been staying with their aunt for a week, ever since Father had become unwell and disappeared into his bedroom, and Mother has told them they would be going away to let him get better. Hugh and Pat are too young to notice much, but John worries about his father.

He sees little of his father normally; Roland Crooke has an important job in London, leaves early to go to it and comes back late. But on Saturdays they go for walks, and on Sundays there is church and Sunday lunch, cooked by Millie the maid.

Aunt Phyllis's new telephone rings, and John hears a low conversation conclude before Aunt Phyll comes into the living room.

"That was Mummy, darling, she'd like Johnson to take you, Pat and Hugh home now."

"Goody, does that mean Daddy's better?"

"Run along now, John, Smithson is packing your things."

A red-eyed Millie lets him into the house in the Berkhamsted High Street which is home and gives him a hug. John suddenly feels very cold. The house is silent, apart from a low murmur of conversation from the living room. Millie gently pushes him into the living room, which is full of grownups dressed in black.

Conversation stops. The vicar steps forward, puts a hand not unkindly on his shoulder and says briskly, "Now then, John, you're going to have to be brave. Your father's died, and you are now the man of the house. So, no tears, there's a good lad. Your mother will be rely-

ing on you."

So, John finds himself as a 35-year-old in the second half of 1955 bouncing down a red-hued laterite road in a cheap clone of a Land Rover with a languidly chatty driver, two bodyguards and an excitable Scots terrier called, with great imagination, Blackie. Perhaps his thoughts drift back to another life on the other side of the world and the events which have brought him here.

John is a child of the First World War, which decimated the male population of Western Europe. Two of his three uncles were killed at the battle of the Somme and his own father survived serious wounding and illness at Gallipoli. John is born in 1920, in a Britain much changed after the social and economic hardships of the War. His father, Roland Crooke, is a senior civil servant in the Ministry of Health. He is descended from a long line of Anglo-Irish minor aristocracy dating back to the 17th Century, while John's mother Edith ("Mig") comes from a family of civil servants in India and has lost her only brother at the battle of Mons in the early years of that War.

By the 1900s, the Crookes' wealth, land and title have all gone. Roland's father, William, was a colonial civil servant in India but retired early to devote his life to researching Indian folklore. Unusually for the time, William insisted on equal credit going to his Indian collaborator and as a result, his name is still highly respected in Indian ethnographic circles.

Perhaps because of this, William was unpopular with his fellow "Heaven Born" white servants of the Raj and seems not to have got on very well with his sons either. His sons Elliott and William wrote extensively to their mother from France before their deaths in 1916, but not, apparently, to their father, and nowhere refer to him.

So, John is born in 1920, into the a middle-class family wrecked by the First World War. Like many such families, the Crookes are struggling to find out where they now belong, in a Britain with full male and partial female suffrage and divided by growing class warfare.

John and his parents move to Berkhamsted in the early 1920s. It is a prosperous market and commuter town with good rail links to London, where Roland works as a civil servant. John's brothers Hugh and Pat are born in 1923 and 1927. Their house in the High Street is owned outright, unusually for the time, and will be a vital part of the family's battle for survival.

In 1930, this family, seemingly establishing itself in the new interwar world, is hit by tragedy. Roland, having recovered from his war wounds and associated illnesses, contracts meningitis and dies within weeks.

John and his brothers are sent away when Roland becomes ill, and not allowed back until after his death. None of them ever forget this bewildering act of unintentional cruelty which prevented them from bidding him farewell.

Roland's death is a financial as well as an emotional disaster for Mig and the boys. The post war welfare state does not yet exist, nor are occupational pensions generally available. Medical care and education are all payable in this self-help culture.

But their secret weapon is the submerged middle-class self-help network or mafia which seems to swing into action at times of trial for this group in society. Mig was helped to sweat the asset of the house she had been left by letting rooms in it to other, more marginal members of the class.

Despite having no other apparent income, Mig employs a maid and pays school fees for John and Pat at Berkhamsted school, also patronised at the time by the family of the author Graham Greene and the composer Anthony Hopkins. Hugh, John's middle brother, seems to have received special treatment by way of a scholarship to Cheltenham College, and later to Emmanuel College, Cambridge. Hugh eventually joins the British Council and ends his career as the Cultural Attaché at the British Embassy in Washington.

We know of at least two families, the Martins and the Warrens, who were closely engaged with the Crookes at this time. Mig had lived with the Martins when growing up, and it seems likely that they offered financial support. The young Crooke boys spend a series of happy summer holidays at a farm on the Dorset coast with the Warrens and their children of equivalent ages. Each year a new and more complicated water-borne contraption is unveiled, with names like the "Pushme-pullyou", and the boys would search out new laid eggs in the barns of the farm.

Fig 6: Edith (Mig) with (l to r) Hugh, Pat and John pictured in 1928

So, this is, for the time, a highly unconventional household consisting of a widow, three sons and a maid. John is now the man of the house, and he, Hugh and Pat are protective of their diminutive but determined mother. John seems to be given or have assumed the role of provider, in that having taken School Certs (modern day A levels) in 1938 he, unlike Hugh and Pat, does not go on to higher education. John shoulders this burden without complaint, and also begins a lifelong love of amateur dramatics which does much to sustain him in later life. By 1938, the threat of war is looming once again over Britain. The Munich agreement of that year deferred this risk at the expense of Czechoslovakia's integrity, but by May 1939 it is imminent enough for John to join the Territorial Army as a reserve soldier in the 5th Battalion, Bedfordshire and Hertfordshire Regiment. In August 1939 he started work , at the Medical Sickness Annuity and Life Assurance Society.

On 25 August 1939 John's unit is formally mobilised and he is a full-time soldier by the time war is declared on 3 September. He is 19 years old.

Reflection: His father's early death means that John is thrust into the role of head of the family in waiting. Therefore, he doesn't go into higher education, but into an unexciting job which will earn money to keep the family afloat. He does his patriotic duty by volunteering for the Territorial Army, but maybe he also looked on it as an escape from his tedious new job. He was certainly up for excitement; he also volunteered for the new Commando unit and as a Paratrooper but was not asked to serve with either. In missing out on higher education, John is like Mary (see below), but unlike her, he doesn't seem to mind.

CHAPTER 3

Phoney War

During his basic training, John lodges with a retired police constable called George. Every evening after his wife has made them their tea, George gets my father to dress in his uniform, makes sure he has the price of a pint and then they walk deliberately and slowly to one of the nearest pubs (a different one every time, for reasons which will become obvious).

Once inside, they buy their drinks, and approach the dart board. If it's in use, John and George stand for a time watching proceedings. Then George suggests that the gallant young soldier is shortly to be posted overseas to an uncertain future, and could they play with the occupants for a round of drinks? John is under strict instructions to throw his darts off the board because George is a deadly accurate shot. It never takes long to beat the bemused dart players and be bought their round of beer, and if nobody else can be persuaded to try their hand, they move on to the next pub and repeat the exercise. John claims that George and he only ever had to pay for one drink in any one pub. The irony is that in due course he will get sent overseas, there to face major tribulations and the proximity of death, and he must have remembered this time as a golden prelude to his suffering.

In the autumn of 1939, there is a gradually dawning realisation that war is imminent, only 20 odd years since the last one, the war to end wars, finished. John has never been a top scholar or athlete and it is his younger brother Hugh who has been picked for intellectual advancement at a top public school and Cambridge college. We know that he is a committed Anglican and has literary and dramatic interests. He has a girl friend or friends, one of whom is serious enough for the relationship to have survived the war and his imprisonment, in some form (he talks much later about having had to tell her it was over when he and Mary Pagden got together).

John's younger brother, Pat, remembers meeting John during his training with a friend called Popeye and having tea with these two glamorous uniformed figures. Popeye was a First War veteran who must have despaired at the thought of having to go back to armed conflict, but may have been the figure John remembers taking the raw recruits through weapons training with the words "What we're goin' on with now is... loadin' and aimin'".

So John is pretty much an ordinary recruit, like thousands now entering the army as Britain mobilises against the Nazi threat. The first war with its attendant horrors is well within living memory; John lost two uncles at the Somme offensive, and this picture would have been repeated across households all over Britain. But there is almost complete national unanimity of opinion that Hitler and his allies represent an evil which must be confronted. Max Hastings, in "Chastise", his book about the Dambusters' raid, notes that this clarity about what Britain is fighting against isn't matched by similar unanimity about what they are fighting for, at least until the latter part of the war, when the publication of the Beveridge report generates much cross class discussion about the need to create a society worthy of the sacrifices made by the British people.

Over the following months, John's regiment is shuffled round the country in response to training needs or perceived threat. He is chosen, as he could have expected to be, for officer training and commissioned in May 1940 (still only 19, don't forget). That summer, something approaching hysteria seizes Britain; for some reason, the threat of parachutists, linked to a mysterious 5th Column (the term comes from the Spanish Civil War, when a Nationalist general besieging the capital boasted of having four columns under his command, but a fifth in Madrid) was particularly gripping, and in July, the newly commissioned 2nd Lt John Crooke has, as his first command, the job of leading a reserve party to a "special vigilance operation" around Coltishall Aerodrome in Norfolk. Needless to say, and possibly entirely because of their special vigilance, no parachutists were spotted. Once the threat of invasion is over at the end of 1940, John and his men know that they will be sent overseas; the only questions are when and where. It will be another year before the battalion leaves the UK for service abroad in October 1941.

Fig 7: 2nd Lt John Crooke, aged 19, May 1940

During this period, there are letters home from John which give a flavour of an anxious young man marching his men from pillar to post and back again and speculating about where he will end up. Above all, he does not want to let his men, his regiment, or his family down.

In February 1941 he writes, "*If they go on at this rate some-*

thing or someone is going to crack up; they're bound to, and I hope it isn't me" and *"I do hope the tropics will give me some colour; I can't be a pale face all my life".*

In May 1941, the battalion is training as part of a brigade and division for its expected role in North Africa or the Middle East. John commands the signals platoon, responsible for the battalion's communications, and his happiest time is when he is allowed to take his 30 signallers away for platoon level training in June 1941. *"It did more good than weeks in camp with most of the platoon on fatigues most of the time… It definitely improved the 'esprit de corps' of the platoon and taught them a lot. They were all loth to return to camp but were really happy and fit."* This may have been something to do with the fact that John sent them off to the pub every night, but he didn't miss out, for *"I soon discovered that the Rector's daughters were two charming girls I had met at the Officers' dance at Atherstone. So, I naturally spent Sunday evening from 4 till 10.30 with them, and they taught me tennis!"*

Reflection: We started this chapter with John as a newly enlisted soldier; we end it with him on the eve of departure for war as an officer commanding 30 or so other soldiers, but still only 21 years old. At the end of that year, 1941, he will be about to be pitched into a military disaster and a period of appalling captivity which will almost cost him his life.

CHAPTER 4

The Real Thing

It's dinner time on the USS West Point – "chow time" as the cheery US mess orderlies shout to the queuing squaddies from the Beds and Herts. They move along the chow line expectantly; the food on the West Point is good and makes up for the dreadful sleeping accommodation they must put up with. Corporal Henderson, who in civilian life had been a Communist shop steward, is chatting to his fellow diarist Corporal Lello at the head of the line as they move towards where they are expecting the potatoes to be. They find a pile of white grains, which the spoon wielding orderly tells them is… rice! The men queuing behind them have seen it too. Several have served in India and seen the Indian sepoys eating it, but it's not food for Englishmen. Rice pudding, fair enough, but for dinner? The mutterings of discontent grow louder, and the chow orderlies start looking nervously at each other. Henderson knows how these things works and gets up on a table. He tells the men he'll find an officer and sort things out. Almost immediately the battalion adjutant is there, conferring with Henderson and US Navy quartermaster. The overcrowded ship sailing through tropical heat cannot afford a mutiny and the rice is swiftly withdrawn in favour of instant mashed potato…. It doesn't appear again.

Finally, after many false starts, 5th Beds and Herts is placed under orders to move overseas in September 1941 and sets sail at the end of October. Days before, John is promoted to first lieutenant with others who had completed 18 months as subalterns.

As far as it is possible to tell, when John's battalion left Liverpool at the end of October 1941, it was bound for the Middle East, either to reinforce the existing Allied positions in North Africa or possibly as part of a new offensive elsewhere. This was, after all, what they had been trained for during the last months; as mobile mechanised infantry fighting in desert conditions. Within weeks, however, their heavy kit and vehicles, traveling in the SS Bonnikom, had been sunk by a German U-boat off the coast of South Africa, the start of a chaotic process which would end with no part of their original job description being true, and with the ignominious surrender of the battalion.

The Beds and Herts are travelling on the SS *Reina del Pacifico*, launched in 1931, and until the outbreak of war, the pride of the Pacific Steam Navigation Company which ran services from Liverpool to the West Coast of South America via the Panama Canal. In 1936 she completes the journey to Valparaiso in 26 days and is the largest and fastest motor liner of her age. She was converted into a troopship at the outbreak of war and painted matt grey.

Conditions on board are not those her peacetime passengers would have recognised. Many more troops are carried than the peace time traveller complement. As an officer John shares a single berth cabin with an extra bunk levered in, but other ranks are crammed in much more tightly. Catering and recreation are kept along pre-war class lines with officers using first class facilities, and other ranks those for the lower classes; 3rd class and steerage.

10 days later, the young soldiers of the 5th Beds and Herts are standing on the dock in Halifax, Nova Scotia. It is 9 November 1941. They have already endured 10 days Atlantic crossing in the *Reina*, travelling in storm racked seas from Liverpool in a convoy braving the U-boat menace. The overcrowding and misery have been so bad that they look with foreboding at their next ride, a short walk away.

It is the *USS West Point*. Unlike the *Reina*, this former liner (*SS America*) has been converted into a fully-fledged armed troop transport of the US Navy. Its gleaming white paintwork is now a dull grey. It has anti-aircraft guns located fore, aft and midships, and sandbags and life rafts are piled around its super-structure. The glass of the big windows in the superstructure is obscured by racks of "standee" bunks. These are racks of 6 bunks, bolted together with 18 inches between them, and there are more in the holds of the *West Point*. There is so little room in these rows of bunks when all are occupied that turning over must be done by agreement. There are more bunks in the holds of the ship. One also houses the ship's desalination machinery, which is so loud that the troops must resort to sign language to communicate.

These dreadful contraptions are for the privates, and cor-porals. Sergeants and officers get a bit more space, but even junior officers like John are billeted in single cabins with an extra bunk crammed in them. Thankfully, though, the senior officers, who in this case include Major General Beckwith, the commander of 18th Division are all accommodated more ap-propriately for their status...

The West Point at Sea
Taken by a New Zealand
Airforce Hudson bomber

Fig 8: The former SS America in her US naval uniform

All told, the *West Point*, which as the liner *SS America* car-ried 1202 passengers in varying degrees of comfort from first class to steerage, is now going to be home for the next two months to over 7000 men. As a US Navy ship, it is dry, so the troops will have no rum ration - nor will the officers have their whisky sodas. But they will have lots of food which in terms of quantity and novelty they have not seen hitherto in a rationed England. John remembers ice cream as being plentiful, but less welcome to his men is the appearance of rice as a main meal carbohydrate. They have only ever encountered it as a sort of milky pudding, and it causes a near mutiny. This is an irony beyond imagining, given their later captivity.

In the holds accommodating many of the men the heat, as the ship travels south towards Cape Town, becomes almost unbearable, even though they strip naked. One hold also houses the ship's desalination plant, which makes a noise so loud the men there can't hear themselves speak.

Although the US is technically still neutral in the war, President Roosevelt and Winston Churchill have signed a treaty committing the US to help the UK with logistical support, and the *West Point* is part of a large 6 ship convoy, escorted by heavy US naval forces, which is carrying the British Army's 18th Infantry Division, recruited mostly in East Anglia. At this point in November 1941, the convoy's destination has become the port of Basra in Southern Iraq, where they are to reinforce British positions in the Middle East. On board the *West Point* are two full battalions of troops and the divisional commander plus staff.

The *West Point* takes just over a month to reach Cape Town from Halifax, via Trinidad, arriving on 10 December. By that time, unknown to him, John's fate has been settled. On the 7th of December, the Japanese air force attacks the US Pacific Fleet at Pearl Harbour and destroys most of it. The following day Japanese ground troops land in South East Thailand and North East Malaya. These are hardened troops, including elements of the elite Imperial Guard, who have been practicing for this operation in Hainan island since June 1941.

British and Commonwealth forces in Malaya are commanded by Lieutenant General Arthur Percival. Wartime photographs of him surrendering show him to be a tall man in long shorts with a toothbrush moustache and no chin. He is a decorated First World War hero, with a Military Cross, Croix de Guerre, and a DSO, after which he served in Ireland where he acquired a brutal reputation among the Irish fighters and survived two assassination attempts.

In Malaya Percival has inherited a chaotic planning situation with forces spread around the Malay peninsula in penny packets protecting RAF bases, those forces themselves ill equipped and undertrained, lacking any armoured support (the tanks having been sent off to Russia) and only two thirds of the fighter aircraft Percival reckons he needs.

He does not, however, feel that defences along the north shore of Singapore island, which might have delayed the Japanese advance were necessary or even good for morale, and refuses to build them.

Percival has two plans to pre-emptively invade southern Thailand and secure potential invasion ports there, which he has been refused War Office permission to implement before Pearl Harbour for fear of upsetting the Japanese and Thai governments. However, the British Government has dispatched *HMS Prince of Wales* and *HMS Repulse*, two of its most powerful warships, to provide a naval shield. Undeterred by the running aground of their escorting aircraft carrier which thus removed his air cover, Admiral Tom Phillips sails his squadron towards the Japanese invasion fleet on 10 December. Both ships are promptly sunk, with the loss of almost all hands, and Japanese aircraft go on to destroy over half of all RAF planes in Malaya over three days, generating complete air superiority. Six weeks later John arrives in Singapore.

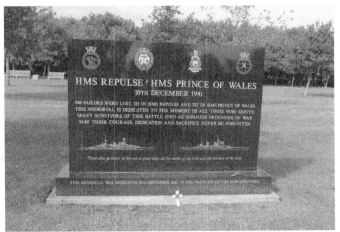

Fig 9: The Singapore memorial to the sinking of Repulse and Prince of Wales

So how did a 20-year-old insurance clerk from Berkhamsted come to be about to participate in one of the worst defeats ever suffered by the British Empire? To answer that question, we must look at how that empire came to include the Malay peninsula and its peoples.

Reflection: I must have been through the events described here dozens of times, and I still find it hard to understand how Britain got to the point of dispatching a full division of troops lightly trained for desert warfare in North Africa or the Middle East to the tropical conditions of Malaya and Singapore, when it was already clear that defeat was inevitable. But it did, and some of the answer may lie in the following chapter.

CHAPTER 5

How the British came to rule Malaya

The first inhabitants of the "Malay" peninsula and the island of Borneo were aboriginal peoples known in the Malay language which developed later, as "Orang Asli" or original people. These were the Senoi and Semang people in the peninsula and Dayak, Iban and Dusun/Kadazan in Borneo. They are subsistence farmers and hunters with animist cultures.

From the 7th Century CE, Chinese travellers' accounts refer to people calling themselves "orang Melayu" (Malay people) as the dominant population in the peninsula. Myth has it that they are Polynesian in origin, coming to the region on long range trading journeys, but proper research indicates that they were descended from the Cham people of Cambodia.

Early Malay society was heavily influenced by Hindu culture and religion and strong trading links developed with India and China. Between the 7th and 13th centuries, much of the peninsula was under the suzerainty of the Hindu-Buddhist empire of Srivijaya. Its hold on local rulers gradually weakened under attacks from the Cholas of Southern India and the growing influence of Islam

In 1402, a Srivijayan prince called Parameswara established himself in the port of Melaka and converted to Islam. His Sultanate acted as the conduit for Islam to spread throughout the peninsula and replaced Srivijaya as the dominant power. All the current sultanates on the peninsula, around 1500, derive from this period; along with the language, culture, and customs we now know as Malay.

At the same time, Western European interest in the area was growing strongly because of spices. These, especially black pepper, were prized as preservatives of meat and concealers of rotten taste and were to be found in the Molucca and Celebes island groups (now Maluku and Sulawesi) in what is now eastern Indonesia. The resurgent Ottoman Turkish empire blocked the overland route, so Portuguese and Dutch merchants developed sea routes round the Cape of Good Hope and Indian ocean to the straits of Melaka and then the spice islands to the east.

Western traders established a growing presence, and in 1511 Portuguese merchants with armed mercenaries evicted Sultan Mahmud Shah from his port of Melaka. Thus, was the first European colony achieved. Mahmud Shah moved to Johor, at the Southern end of the peninsula, from where his dynasty continued to be involved in the history of Malaya.

The Portuguese takeover in Melaka followed a playbook which was used by the Dutch and British also. Essentially it involved taking sides in local disputes, allegedly to preserve peaceful commerce, with the outcome being enhanced powers and influence for the intervening merchants and administrators.

The Dutch East India Company did this in the spice islands and in Java and Sumatra, on the other side of the Melaka straits, throughout the 16th and 17th centuries. By 1662 they had a network of alliances and trading posts in what is now Indonesia and were strong rivals to Portugal for control of the spice trade. In that year they allied themselves to Mahmud Shah's descendant as Sultan of Johor and took Melaka.

The British East India Company had India as its focus, and by the mid- 18th Century had still not managed to get a permanent foothold in the Peninsula or the spice trade. This was irking the Company's directors, whose opium trade with China required a secure port on the sea route between India and China.

But in 1786 Francis Light changed all that. He had served in the East India Company army with little distinction and was now an enterprising country trader. This was the EIC description of a free-lancer who was based in India, but travelled in the surrounding area, having raised some trading capital, trying to make money in the local markets. Light had been doing this in and around the Straits of Melaka and could see the benefits that the Dutch and Portuguese had derived from controlling permanent trading bases. He spoke fluent Malay and used this and his connections to negotiate the lease from the Sultan of Kedah of the island of Penang together with a block of territory on the mainland opposite the island. In the normal acts of flattery, he named the island's main settlement Georgetown, after the then King, and the mainland holding Province Wellesley, after the Company's Governor General in India, Arthur Wellesley, later Duke of Wellington.

And so began the march of Empire. It does seem that at this stage the main British interest was in secure trade and exploitation of resources, but while this acquisition was not part of any imperial masterplan, the mere presence of the British created tensions and opportunities which would lead inevitably to further expansion.

Thus… In 1795, the British took the port of Melaka over from the local Dutch administration in order, apparently, to prevent it being taken by the French, who had recently defeated the Dutch in Europe. In 1815 the defeat of Napoleon resulted in Britain meekly handing Melaka back to the Dutch, whereupon its British Governor travelled south and negotiated the lease of Singapore. Everything got tidied up in 1826, when Britain and the Netherlands swapped the British colony of Benkulen in Sumatra for Melaka.

At a stroke, Britain, in the form of the East India Company, now controlled three ports (Penang, Melaka and Singapore) on the Melaka straits and thus achieved strategic domination. These three ports were formally created the Straits Settlements under the control of the EIC. As free ports, they offered low taxes and the security of British administration.

With this bridgehead, local rulers in the peninsula began to see the Company as an attractive counterweight to Siam, to whom they owed suzerainty, and as an ally in their disputes with each other. This was the same pattern that had emerged in India itself and which there, had led to the Company becoming a dominant power.

British and other European merchants and traders flocked to the settlements, even though they also functioned as penal colonies for dangerous Indian criminals. They invested in the Chinese run tin mining industry which had begun in the states of Perak, Negeri Sembilan and Selangor. Tin had probably been mined in the Malay Peninsula for centuries, but by the mid-19th century it had become an important element of many alloys, including that used in cans for preserving food. Malay subsistence farmers however were highly reluctant to work at the dangerous and poorly paid work of tin mining. Melaka became the centre of the mining industry from the 1820s onwards and through it flooded tens of thousands of male migrants from the southern provinces of China, whose lawlessness and poverty made them more than ready to accept the privations of tin mining for the pay offered by tin mining merchants.

These merchants began to demand ever more loudly British intervention to secure the right climate for their investments to prosper. Local British administrators, in their dispatches back to Calcutta and London, strike a rather irritated tone as they recount these demands. In parallel, they bemoan the constant feuding of local Malay rulers and their pleas for help before shrugging their shoulders and recommending intervention. Perak was the first state to move under British suzerainty with the Treaty of Pangkor in 1874, which established a British Resident at the Sultan's court. The Sultan was required to take the Resident's advice on all matters save religion and custom. The British had successfully adopted this approach in India, and it worked just as well for them in the Malay Peninsula.

The tin mining industry exploded thanks to the greater security offered by British indirect rule. The Chinese miners consumed large quantities of opium, which increased tax revenues, and some married local Malay women to create the Baba and Nyonya communities. Eventually, they felt secure enough to import brides and then teachers for the resulting children and a large, settled community developed, creating one of the strengths and tensions of modern Malaysia. This community created businesses, banks and insurance companies which dominated the local economy, in partnership with the big Western companies. In general Malays did not participate in this economic activity, and by the end of the 19th century they were in a minority in its heartlands of Selangor, Perak, Negeri Sembilan and the Straits Settlements.

At this time, the Chinese were joined by numbers of largely Tamil workers from Southern India. They were indentured (i.e. contracted to work for their employers until the costs of their passage had been paid off) workers whose passages had been paid by western companies piling into the new rubber industry. The first rubber seeds were smuggled from Brazil to Kew Gardens and then the Malay peninsula in 1877. Demand for rubber soared when the air-filled rubber tyre was invented for cars, making them a viable mass transport option. By 1930, Malaya was producing roughly half the world's supply.

As with tin, Malays either really did not, or were casually presumed not to, want to work in the production process which involved outdoor work tapping rubber trees and collecting the resultant latex and indoor work processing the latex into basic rubber sheet. Roughly half the production was in the hands of small-scale smallholders, mostly Chinese. The other half was controlled by a range of western companies and individual entrepreneurs, and these turned to Southern India for their source of labour. Thousands of indentured labourers arrived in the last years of the 19th century, further transforming the population mix of the peninsula.

By the early 20th century Malays made up a bare majority of the population, but the Chinese were 30% and Tamils a little under 10% of the inhabitants of the peninsula. More importantly, they were only marginally involved in the frantic economic activity based around rubber and tin. They were seen by the British as cheerful but lazy, content to sit in their kampungs and wait for the coconuts to fall.

The traditional Malay rulers were maintained and subsidised by Britain and Malays took all the higher level administrative, military and police positions not held by the British. Despite this there developed among the Malays in the early 20th century a strong feeling of discontent with their lack of economic and political power.

The Chinese migrants had arrived penniless but seeking family and education ties through mutual aid societies based on the area of China they came from. These Hokkien, Hakka, Foo Chow organisations, largely indistinguishable from gangs, provided education, social life savings, banking, and insurance to the Chinese communities.

The British population grew as the British presence established itself, but never became one of settlement, unlike in South and East Africa, but like India itself, which had actively discouraged the growth of an Anglo Indian or Eurasian settler community.

By the time of the Second World War, therefore, "British Malaya" was an economically successful producer of rubber and tin with a mixed population not sharing equally in the fruits of the prosperity generated by the primary products it produced.

Reflection: Like many other parts of the world absorbed into the British Empire, Malaya/Malaysia's journey from a collection of sultanates trading and jostling for influence can be seen as a succession of un-planned events ending up with the peninsula falling into Britain's lap, much to its slightly irritated surprise. There genuinely does not seem to have been a master plan for the process, which doesn't make it any better, but does recognise the role of chance and opportunity. Britain's arrogant assumption of its innate superiority, which underpinned this expansion of its power, was about to come badly unstuck.

CHAPTER 6

A House of Cards

John is standing holding a surfboard in the waist-deep water off Kalk Bay, a seaside resort near Cape Town. It is 10 December, and on the other side of the world the pride of the Royal Navy, the Prince of Wales and the Repulse, are being sunk by Japanese torpedo bombers. This event alone has condemned him to surrender and imprisonment, but he does not yet know it. He does know that he loves surfing and doesn't want to stop doing it. It is high summer in Cape Town, and he is being shown round by a local white family, who have brought him here to try it. The journey from Liverpool, via the West Indies, to Freetown and Cape Town has taken nearly six weeks, in increasing heat and discomfort, while censored news about the war has got worse and worse.

These few days respite, he knows, presage huge uncertainty about his future and that of his men. Rumours have been flying around about their destination; some say Basra in Iraq, which would fit the role for which they have trained – mobile infantry in desert warfare. Others say they will be going to the Middle East to protect oil wells in the Caucasus. Some poor deluded souls say they are bound for Malaya, where things are not going well, despite its impregnable naval base at Singapore. But this is clearly nonsense; they have not been trained for tropical, jungle warfare and haven't got the right equipment.

John puts all this on one side. His generous hosts are taking him out to dinner and a concert. Tomorrow the CO has called an Orders Group, and he may learn more then. He's sure that the top brass knows what it's doing...

Despite defeat after defeat in France and the surrender of the British Expeditionary Force, the British population of Malaya remains largely complacent and unaware of the looming clouds of their own demise. One of the reasons for this is their misplaced confidence in Singapore, the jewel in the Imperial Crown. Singapore is, by the start of the second world war, the home to a vast Naval Base. Originally, the base was to be the home of a British Pacific Fleet, but it has never fulfilled that role. By the time of its completion in the late 1930s, Britain is unable to afford its original grand design of separate fleets in the Atlantic and Pacific oceans but has instead opted to keep the bulk of its assets in Britain and in the Mediterranean, in theory at least able to respond to emergencies in both the Atlantic and Pacific. The reality of war will prove different.

So, the function of the base at the start of World War 2 is to act as the temporary home for ships deployed there from other places. Planning for the Army and Air Force assets in Malaya seems to have proceeded entirely independently from the Navy. The RAF has chosen to build several airfields throughout Malaya, which the Army has then been forced to provide garrisons to protect. This lack of coordination bedevilled military efforts before and during the conflict.

In addition, the island stands well behind the home islands and North Africa in the queue for resources. For example, all 366 tanks there were taken away in 1940 and sent to Russia, and only two thirds of the fighter aircraft that local commanders have asked for have been supplied. None of the new Spitfire fighters are available, and numbers of their less glamorous Hurricane sisters only start arriving when it is too late. The aircraft that are available are largely obsolete planes called things like Wildebeest and Buffalo, names not designed to instil confidence...

British, Indian, and Australian troops reinforcing the garrison, including John and his comrades, are largely raw recruits with extraordinarily little relevant training in jungle fighting.

Only the Argyll and Sutherland Highlanders, manned largely by tough Glaswegians and resident in Singapore for several years, is up to the sort of close quarter combat they are going to encounter in oppressive heat and thick forest. And that is because their commander insists on taking them into the Malayan jungle to practice these things, much to the disapproval of the other battalion commanders. But despite all this, there is an entirely unjustified belief that the Base is impregnable, and that the Japanese were nothing like the highly competent and battle-hardened troops they were. Japan had been fighting a campaign in China for many years, and unlike the British their military worked as one.

On 10 December, John's convoy reached Cape Town. This was the day of the sinking of the two British battleships and two days after the Japanese invasion of Malaya. The decision was taken to divert the convoy to Singapore.

John writes the last of a series of scrupulously self-censored letters to Mig on 16 December, having left Cape Town (although he never mentions its name) after 3 days of idyllic sounding leave, during which he learns how to surf:

> *"There's definitely a knack about surfing, and I only had about three ("or 4" crossed out) really successful turns, but my word! when you do get a successful run, when you hit the breaking wave with your board in just the right place and it sweeps you right in shore, it is the most completely satisfying feeling I have ever experienced".*

Surfers down the ages will second that emotion, from a 21-year-old on his first trip outside Britain, maybe just starting to feel the first premonitions of impending disaster. When would he feel this free again?

John is punctilious in his efforts to censor his letters, even going so far as to cut out the ship's name from the headed notepaper he was using. It's ironic to read elsewhere (in From the

Woodlands to the Jungle, by Martin Fryer) a detailed letter from a Cape Town resident to the wife of another officer about the battalion's stay in the port, complete with names and dates

There are also, in John's correspondence, constant themes of longing for home and lack of contact with his family and country. He seems not to have had any mail at all from home during the trip out, though these letters of his obviously got back to Mig. His are peppered with requests to write, to make sure that the right address was on any letters written to him and speculation about what was going on at home, like this:

"(I hope) you will have had some fun opening (my letters) in front of the drawing room fire with Tinker and Benjie curled up on the rug"

"I say, won't I be unbearable when I come home?- all "builders of empire" and bridge-playing- completely constructed of marble from the neck up. Shoot 'em down, me boy, shoot 'em down!"

On the day John writes this letter (16 December 1941), the island port of Penang on the North West coast of Malaya falls to the Japanese Army. Shortly before this happens, Penang's remaining European residents are put on two ships and sent south to Singapore. Very few Asians are on these boats; the British colonial power is saving its own and leaving the local population to fend for itself. This shameful act is repeated throughout the peninsula.

"I betrayed my Malay Gardener. He cut my hedges, watered my flowers, cut and rolled my tennis lawn and brushed up the leaves that blew down from the tree. I betrayed my round, fat amah, who liked me, and amused me with her funny ways. I betrayed my Hokkien cook, who had a wife and four lovely children, whom he always kept beautifully dressed on the money he earned from me. I betrayed "Old Faithful", our No2 Boy, who knew no word of English or Malay and padded round the house silently in bare feet, always working cheerfully. I betrayed the cad-

die who carried my bag, searched for my ball, and always
backed my game with a sporting bet. I betrayed all the lit-
tle helpless babies with their almond eyes and soft black
shining heads. From the college student to the Tamil coolie
who swept the street, I betrayed them all." (Leslie Froggatt
Memoir).

There are occasional acts of self-sacrifice on the part of
Europeans who stayed to face the Japanese music, but more typical is the reaction of Penang's Chief Surveyor, who bemoaned
the "loss of his tiger hunting trophies, which cut him more
deeply than anything". By contrast, some of the abandoned
servants hid silverware and other valuables for their escaping
employers and dutifully returned them three and a half years
later. The shameful behaviour of the colonisers makes it even
more humbling, and surprising, that they would be, largely,
welcomed back at the end of the war. John will find himself a
beneficiary of this generous hearted approach and will have remembered his own betrayal by his government. Had the Japanese occupiers adopted a more civilised approach towards local
non-Malay residents, things could have been vastly different.

It is just before the convoy reaches Cape Town that the
decision is taken to switch its destination from Basra to Singapore. The British general staff must know by now that the
position in Malaya is lost. Two capital ships have been sunk and
most of the RAF's diminished complement of Buffalo, Wilde-
beests, and other obsolete aircraft, have been shot down or destroyed on the ground. The combined Empire forces have failed
to hold up the Japanese advances down the west and east coasts
of Malaya.

Japanese tactics have largely consisted of driving down
the west and east coast highways, which have been consider-
ately left intact by the retreating British and Indian forces, until
they come to a roadblock. They then peel off the road on either
side of the block, advance through the forest or rubber planta-

tion on either side and appear again behind the blocking troops, inducing panic in the inexperienced soldiers and a further retreat. Or they just drive straight through using their light tanks-which the British troops don't themselves have since Churchill has sent them all to Russia.

Despite all this, Churchill decides to commit the 18th Division to the slaughter that the Malayan campaign has become. He does so because he needs to show that the British Empire is an equal partner to the Soviet Union, currently suffering huge losses against the German offensive, and to the United States, which is reeling from the Pearl Harbour disaster. And that it is willing to commit as much as it can to retaining its imperial jewel at Singapore.

At Cape Town, the Division of which John's battalion is part was split. Two thirds of it, including the 5th Beds and Herts, is sent to India, for belated and irrelevant hot weather training, but a third brigade is sent direct to Singapore by a clearly panicking War Office, and arrived on 13 January. By this time, the Japanese advance has engulfed most of the Malay peninsula, and 53 Brigade is flung into action in Johore, the mainland state next to Singapore. To quote the brigade diary; "*Very few.... had been in the tropics, and absolutely none had been trained in jungle fighting. They had arrived without transport or guns, which were .... in Bombay*".

Untrained, ill-equipped, and poorly led, the Brigade is cut to pieces by the allegedly inferior Japanese forces, with heavy casualties. News must have reached the remainder of 18th Division about the fate of their comrades.

Meanwhile John's part of the Division arrives in Mumbai/Bombay on 28 December, by which time, Kuala Lumpur, the capital of the Malay States, has fallen. Here some attempt was made to acclimatise the troops through 3 weeks of "*route marches and training in tropical heat*" (5th Beds and Herts War Diary) at Ahmednagar, 250 kilometres inland from Mumbai. It is almost as if the penny has finally dropped amongst the "marble headed" British High Command that they are losing, and frantic efforts are made to bring these, the last reinforcements into Singapore, up to some sort of capable standard.

There are no letters from John surviving from this frantic period of training in India, but we can be sure of the despair he would have felt as he leads his men on a hopeless series of route marches in conditions completely different to those he would find in Malaya. Despite the full-on crisis which now engulfs the British forces, officers in India are still expected to turn up for dinner in the evenings in full mess uniforms and stay drinking until the early hours.

During this time, frantic preparations are being made for the convoy to go to Singapore. *West Point's* draught is too deep to get through the relatively shallow waters around the island. The loss of most of the Malay peninsula means that the convoy will have to sail a wide diversionary route round Sumatra, and even then, will be subject to air attack from the Japanese Air Force, who now have command of the air.

On 19 January 1942, the rest of 18th Division leaves Bombay bound for Singapore. *West Point's* draught has been reduced by taking out fuel and drinking water, but she still must navigate the shallow Sunda Straits, between Sumatra and Java. They do so in bright moonlight but without air attack. During this last leg of the journey, John remembers being subjected to the most appalling lies and misinformation by so-called "Intelligence Officers" in last-minute briefings.

Among the things they are told are that the Japanese soldiers are short-sighted, unable to see at night, and riddled with disease. Their aircraft are said to be poor copies of British ones and made of bamboo, while the soldiers themselves only have small calibre .22 rifles.

Yet, according to a fellow officer of John's, and despite all these disadvantages,

> "*Things seemed to be going so badly that we couldn't imagine how we would be able to arrive in time to do*

any good. No-one on board had seen a jungle or what a Japanese soldier looked like; nor were there any books or pamphlets available which might enlighten us. So, our imaginary schemes and lectures on board had to be based on guesswork, and they were not particularly good guesses either".

There seems to have been a concerted attempt to keep these lambs to the slaughter in happy ignorance of what was awaiting them.

On 29 January, with John's convoy 10 days into its journey from Mumbai, General Percival, the General Officer Commanding Empire troops, gives the order for the remaining troops in Southern Malaya to withdraw to Singapore. The last troops back, on 31 January, are the Argyll and Sutherland Highlanders, who march proudly across the causeway linking the island of Singapore with Johore state behind their two remaining pipers. Then the charges under the causeway are blown. They fail to destroy it, and the simultaneous destruction of the naval base, the imperial pride and joy, is also incomplete.

***Reflection:** The story of Britain sleepwalking into its worst ever military disaster still leaves me open-mouthed. The callous arrogance with which many thousands of men were committed to a campaign which had in effect already been lost, and the arrant racist nonsense they were fed by way of briefing beggars belief. As does the British betrayal of its colonial subjects, whom it had airily assured it would protect. The British commanders were incapable of understanding that who they considered a race of small oriental people could defeat and humiliate them in the way they were about to. And the colonised people who witnessed it would never hold the Empire in the same awe again.*

CHAPTER 7

Defeat

The exhausted group of men, carrying heavy wireless equip-
ment, starts digging in at its exposed position on the shores of the
McRitchie reservoir, the main water supply for the city of Singapore.
They are under the command of Lieutenant John Crooke, who hasn't
slept for two nights.

They are supposed to be relaying to battalion HQ reports from
the rest of Wells Force about the Japanese advance. Little information
is coming in, however, and Battalion HQ itself is falling back towards
the city.

Japanese artillery is firing from the other side of the causeway
and several of John's men are wounded. The noise of the bombard-
ment is ear shattering and constant. Then, well after nightfall on 15
February, the guns fall silent. General Percival has issued an order to
the 90,000 Indian, Australian, and British soldiers in Singapore to
surrender unconditionally.

Having checked his men are as well as can be expected, John
falls into a deep, dreamless sleep, his head pillowed on a stone. He is
not yet 22 years old.

Ten days after leaving Mumbai/Bombay, *West Point* and
Wakefield approach Singapore on 30 January 1942. If John has
any lingering illusions about the situation, they have been
dashed by now. The much-vaunted naval base has been partially
destroyed, and remaining shipping is going in and out of the
commercial harbour next door. There are continuous heavy air
raids, one of which is going on as they dash for port and scores

a direct hit on *Wakefield*. The dock workers are taking cover, so *West Point* is unloaded by her crew and the embarked troops. This doesn't take long since there is no heavy equipment: They are the last ships into Singapore before surrender, and the Division they carry is going into action with just the rifles and light weapons the men carry.

The scene that greets them as they march through Singapore towards their camp at Changi is like something out of Dante's Inferno. The docks are full of civilians and troops of all races, officially or unofficially waiting, who are now crowding round the *West Point* hoping to get on board and out of Singapore. Fires are burning in shattered buildings and groups of deserting troops are roaming the streets, looting shops and bars. Civilian casualties have been heavy, but air raid precautions have been negligible in this impregnable fortress. Many Australian troops have deserted and yell advice at the new reinforcements to save themselves.

Still, John's men march as part of a coherent unit to their quarters at Birdwood Camp, Changi, on the North East corner of the Isle of Wight shaped island of Singapore. What is going through their minds? Among other things, they can see from the retreating troops coming over the causeway that the information they have been fed about the nature and capability of the inferior Japanese troops is outrageously untrue.

The next day (31 January), the Beds and Herts start trying to create a defensive line on the northeast coast around the RAF station at Seletar, which has been abandoned with all its contents intact. All the Division's three Brigades are stationed here, including the 53rd, which is by now more or less finished as a fighting force. They are facing a Japanese force, now less than a mile away across the strait, which has taken six weeks to bundle an army twice its size out of Malaya, and which now has access to countless airfields, ammunition, and British supplies. They control much of the water supply for the island. They are already starting to take reprisals against the local Chinese population and anybody else they deem to be sympathetic to the vanquished colonial power. Thousands of Indian troops have deserted from their British officered regiments and have been used by the Japanese to guard the many prisoners of war already "in the bag". Shelling starts and goes on for the next week.

Amid its attempts to ready itself for its role defending the North East coast of Singapore, the battalion discovers that the maps it has been issued of the Isle of Wight shaped island are indeed of the Isle of Wight, and a corporal with artistic leanings is assigned to create new maps from scratch by tracing the outline of Singapore from a map of the real island they find on a school classroom wall and copying the result for the company commanders.

John's job as signals platoon commander is to keep communications going between the various bits of the battalion and the rest of the Garrison. Over the next two weeks until the final surrender on 13 February 5th Beds and Herts disintegrates as a fighting force, as it is split into smaller and smaller packets of increasingly desperate troops. John's signallers are trying to keep all these bits of his regiment in touch and it is a losing battle - to go with the bigger disaster which is now in its endgame.

The beginning of the end comes on 9th February, when Japanese forces in small boats land in the mangrove swamps on the northwest coast of Singapore. They slice, like a hot knife through butter, through the two Australian army Brigades defending this coast, who cease to fight quite quickly and join the mobs of deserters in the city. Soon their commander, the appalling General Gordon Bennett, will leave Singapore by hijacking a boat at gunpoint, abandoning his troops to captivity.

The Japanese forces now pour across the only partly destroyed causeway. John, his signallers, and the rest of HQ Company are defending the main road from the causeway south to the city against the main Japanese thrust but fail to hold their line. Five officers and many men are killed in this battle, and John's platoon gets caught up in another five days of confused retreating, marching and occasional fighting before the surrender.

The madness includes an officer who had clearly seen too

many westerns snatching up a machine gun and advancing up a hill firing it from the hip before he is swiftly shot, and another officer telling his men that it was every man for himself. One soldier who hears him then spends some hours assembling a group of other men and supplies with the idea of re-crossing the causeway and doing...... what? Luckily for him, the order is speedily cancelled. Finally, a group of men who are resupplied under fire with pay and cigarettes by the regimental chaplain who tries then to get them to pay for them.

On 10 February, Lt Col Rhys Thomas, the CO of the Beds and Herts, faced with the disintegration of the British defences, split his men into two groups. John finds himself in "Wells Force", the half commanded by Major Tom Wells. Their task is to defend the McRitchie reservoir, one of the few remaining water supply sources in Singapore and situated on the high ground to the north of the city. John and a small group of his remaining signallers are in an exposed position as a listening post. Their job is to relay information about Japanese positions back to Battalion HQ. But HQ itself is by now in retreat towards the city.

Before they have the chance to die pointlessly, General Percival issues an order for unconditional surrender at 8.10 pm on 15 February 1942. John's war is over. Later he remembers being unutterably tired and sleeping soundly with his head pillowed on a stone. He is 21. The Beds and Herts have lost 6 officers and somewhere between 26 and 60 men in the two weeks of chaotic fighting. Over the next 3½ years of captivity in the jungles of Thailand, and in Japan itself, more than 300 of their comrades will perish, about half the battalion's original strength.

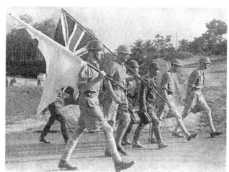

Fig 10: General Percival (centre carrying Union flag) surrendering to underwhelming force.

One hundred and thirty thousand British, Australian, Dutch, Indian and Gurkha troops have been defeated by a Japanese force half that size, which was close to running out of supplies until the final collapse. John and his comrades are Prisoners of War- "in the bag" in the slang of the time.

Reflection: *There is absolutely no doubt that the 18th Division of which John's battalion was part, was committed to the defence of Singapore to show that Britain was committed to its naval base and colony, and to maintain its position as a major Ally. There was certainly no military reason; this was a division untrained for the fighting it would face, with no naval or air support, going into a hopeless position. The definitive futile gesture.*

CHAPTER 8

In the Bag

John is one of 16000 prisoners of war confined in the central square area of the Selarang Barracks. There is little space and they have been there for five days. There are no lavatories and only one water tap. The Japanese Army commander has "requested" that the Allied prisoners sign an undertaking not to escape, following four prisoners having tried to do just that and been recaptured. The senior allied officer has refused on behalf of his men and even the botched execution of the four escapees has failed to change this refusal.

But now men are starting to die from dysentery and related diseases, and in what sounds like a classic compromise, the Japanese general has converted the request into an order, which the British can sign since a declaration under duress doesn't count. Just to make sure, many soldiers sign using the name Micky Mouse or Ned Kelly. Thereafter, occasional escape attempts were made, despite the utter hopelessness of half-starved white prisoners trying to travel many hundreds of kilometres to friendly territory. After the war, John and his comrades are all interviewed by MI9 the agency responsible for POW escapes to find out why they had not tried. I can imagine some of the language used.

The Imperial Japanese Army, having won the Malayan campaign, now has the problem of what to do with the defeated troops of the other side, roughly twice their number. The victorious troops must still overcome the Dutch garrison in present day Indonesia, which they do over the next 6 weeks or so, so the many Indian soldiers who have surrendered to the

Japanese are initially enlisted as guards, then into two incarnations of an Indian National Army, dedicated to Indian independence. The Malay population greet the Japanese arrival warmly. They have been promised unspecified special treatment within the Japanese Greater East Asian Co-Prosperity Sphere and are allowed latitude to develop ideas around a Greater Malaya incorporating Indonesia.

The new prisoners of war are marched through the streets of Singapore to Changi Camp, the largest military settlement in Singapore. The local Malay, Chinese and Indian population, which has suffered extensive casualties from Japanese bombing, is ordered to watch as their former rulers walk in the midday sun, with varying amounts of discipline, to the camp. Some offer water but most just stare in amazement at this humiliation, engineered by a race of people not too dissimilar to themselves. This demolition of the British and Dutch imperial reputation was incredibly important once the war was over.

The largely Chinese population of Singapore is already suffering harsh treatment from the Japanese because of the years of warfare between the two peoples in China itself, and from these origins will spring the resistance force called the Malayan People's Anti-Japanese Army. This in turn will spawn the Malayan Races Liberation Army which will launch the post war Emergency. John will be part of all of this in his post war life.

For now, he is but one of 90000 prisoners being shuffled around Singapore island. At one point, John is very comfortably quartered at an officers' camp with silver service in the mess. One of their first jobs is to build for the Japanese a shrine to their victory, intended as a religious destination for future Japanese visitors to Syonan, as the Japanese term Singapore. This is on three raised stone and concrete platforms, with sloping roofs on timber uprights. A large fountain sits beside the shrine, fed from the same MacRitchie reservoir which John and Wells Force had defended.

In April 1942, the Beds and Herts move to a camp at Sime Road. Here John and another officer, to preserve normality as far as possible, run French classes which they take extremely seriously; thus John (still not 22 years old), rather pompously at a class one evening:

> *"There is too much collusion among the students from the cookhouse area, you will learn more if you work as individuals"* R Rivett (Behind Bamboo)

To which the reasonable muttered response is recorded by Rivett as *"Scary old sod"*. Note the "old".

It is almost a cliché to say that the Japanese approach to treatment of their prisoners of war in the second World War is extremely brutal. Japan is not a signatory to the Geneva Convention, which regulates the treatment of prisoners of war, but around now announces that it will adhere to its provisions. At this stage, the treatment of POWs is not as bad as it later becomes. As far as possible, the Japanese Army uses renegade Indian Army soldiers for guarding duties, who varied greatly in their approach to their former colonisers. The Japanese officers are relatively junior and not of front-line calibre. They are capable of friendly gestures and conversation, but also of the sort of acts of brutality which become commonplace later.

John witnesses two potential (but unidentified) war crimes committed by a Japanese Officer at around this time, contained in Affidavits JC/132 and 89 sworn at the end of the war for the war crimes unit, but the officer seems to have suffered no sanction.

In June, all officers above the rank of Lt Col, from General Percival downwards are sent to Japan. The Japanese want to detach the senior commanders from the rest of the captive troops to minimise the possibility of organised resistance, and to keep the highest value prisoners together as potential bargaining chips.

The remaining officers are immediately faced with a chain of events later known as the Selarang Incident. British and

Australian Army soldiers have been trained to believe that it is their duty to try to escape captivity and resume their service to the crown. Despite the vanishingly small chances of success in doing so, with the nearest free Allied forces a thousand miles away and the obvious difficulty in passing unnoticed, two Australian and two British soldiers do try to escape in August 1942 from the Selarang Barracks in Singapore.

They are rapidly recaptured, and the Japanese make 17000 troops march from Changi to join the remaining soldiers in Selarang. Japanese officers then require British officers on behalf of their men to sign undertakings not to escape.

The Geneva Conventions allow for attempts to escape, and recaptured prisoners are not supposed to be punished for trying to flee. This cuts no ice at all with the Japanese commander. 17000 troops are confined in an area 128 by 210 metres, with no lavatories and one water tap. After three days, the soldiers are still holding out, so the Japanese commander orders the execution of the four escapees. Indian National Army soldiers, in the forced presence of the senior Australian and British officers, fire at the soldiers but fail to kill them with their first volley. Eventually they are dispatched, and the standoff continues for two more days. Men start to die from disease and dehydration, and at this point their commanders order the remaining men to sign, under duress. This they do, but the most popular Australian signature is... Ned Kelly.

Reflection: In retrospect, the 5-6 months between the fall of Singapore and the start of the northward journeys to Thailand were relatively gentle ones for the surrendered troops, despite the Selarang atrocity. British units like the 5ᵗʰ Beds and Herts consolidated their internal organisation and developed messing funds which would provide vital canteen supplies to supplement the poor or non-existent rations provided by the Japanese to the parties sent north to build the railway.

CHAPTER 9

Building the Railway

John lies on his bamboo charpoy in the sleeping hut. It is October 1943. By now he has lost well over a third of his weight when he was captured. Like thousands of others in these monsoon months, he has contracted cholera. Cholera is caught from dirty water and stagnant pools and has already driven a swathe through the camps for Asian labourers, which have none of the support systems the POWs have created for themselves. Now it has taken hold in the Prisoner of War camps, and two thirds of all POW deaths will occur at this time.

The main symptom is catastrophic diarrhoea resulting in dehydration and death, and the only treatment is rehydration. John is being treated with blood donated by fellow prisoners which contains water and salts. It is being donated and fed to him from bamboo buckets being stirred by the prisoners and via bamboo canulae inserted in his arm vein. It saves his life.

By October 1942, with the conquest of South East Asia completed, Japanese attention is on the British forces in India. These include the defeated garrison of Burma which has been ignominiously chased back into India a few months earlier. Japanese forces are being resupplied and reinforced by sea because there is no continuous rail link from Malaya and Thailand through Burma to the front-line adjoining Assam, and the sea lanes are highly vulnerable to attack from US submarines.

There is a pre-war British plan to build this link, from Banpong, west of Bangkok to Thanbyzayat in Burma, which fills in the gap in the existing rail provision. It covers a total distance of 414.9 kilometres and has never gone ahead because it covers terrain which is considered to be impassable. The Japanese High Command now orders its construction and completion within 18 months, working towards a central meeting point from Banpong and Thanbyzayat. They plan initially to use local labour, forced and voluntary, but the scope and intensity of the operation proves to be beyond the capacity of that labour force. The Japanese Commander of the Southern army hits upon the idea of using the huge pool of organised, mostly disciplined, still relatively fit, educated labour sitting in camps in Singapore and Indonesia consuming resources and contributing little to the Japanese war effort. The High Command agree immediately.

Thus, on 17 October 1942 John is waiting at Tanjong Pagar Railway station in Singapore with 63 other men from the Beds and Herts, and others, making a total of 650, the first party of what will ultimately be 50,000 allied slave labourers. They have marched 10 miles in the blazing sun to get here, through the middle of Singapore, as is now usual so that the population get a good look at their humiliated former colonisers The Japanese have told them that they are going to rest camps up country with good food and medical supplies, but it's unlikely that the now 22-year-old John, or the others going, are fooled, especially once they see their transport. As they wait in line on the platform a rattling line of 26 steel cattle wagons trundles into the station. Each wagon takes up to 30 men and their possessions. There is no room to lie down except by organised arrangement of everybody in the wagon, but this is soon worked out.

John says later that the reason so many of his comrades survive their captivity was because of the British regimental system, which largely stayed intact until the end of the war. This was not the case with the American, Australian, and Dutch prisoners, whose survival rates were lower. Under the British system, the regiment is a family, in which all combine for mutual support, and whose resources are shared. In prison camp, it means, for example, that the exact locations of the graves of each man who died along the railway is recorded in a book which also contains the next of kin details for each man.

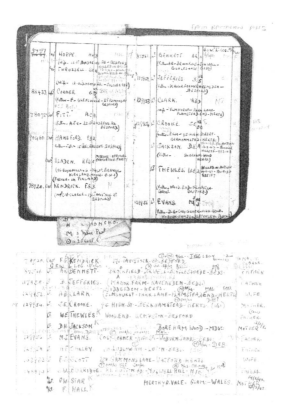

Fig 11: Notebook used to record details of each soldier in 5th Beds
and Herts, with next of kin contacts and burial location if killed. This
was carried by an officer throughout the period of captivity.

By this point in their captivity - over one year in - many POWs are already suffering from dysentery and other vitamin deficiency diseases.

In the hell that is their journey to Thailand, which took five days and four nights, the mutual help took the form of ensuring that those prisoners with the worst diarrhoea are hung out of the sliding doors whenever they are open, and that every opportunity to cook and distribute a meal is taken when the train stops.

On about Day 3, the cattle trucks pass through the North Western state of Kedah and, although at the time he would not have known exactly where he was, John remembers looking out of the right-hand side of the train and seeing a black and white painted bungalow a few hundred meters away on an outcrop of land, with young rubber trees planted all around it. He knew then that he would one day live in that house, and he clung on to that memory through the years of horror which followed.

Fig 12: John's view of the first house seen in 1941. Photo taken in 1993

On 21 October, the shabby band of POWs arrive at the Banpong rail head where the Thai end of the new railway will start.

Banpong is a depot from which troops are sent on up the line of the railway to build its component parts. Conditions are horrific there; monsoon rains have flooded the huts and latrines, so faeces are floating everywhere. Luckily for him, John is instantly sent on with No 2 Party 59 km up the line to Chungkai camp. Chungkai is one of the best camps, with relatively good accommodation, safe bathing, and access to reasonably priced extra foodstuffs. A major hospital is established here.

Fig 13: The route of the railway, with John's locations , with dates plotted on it

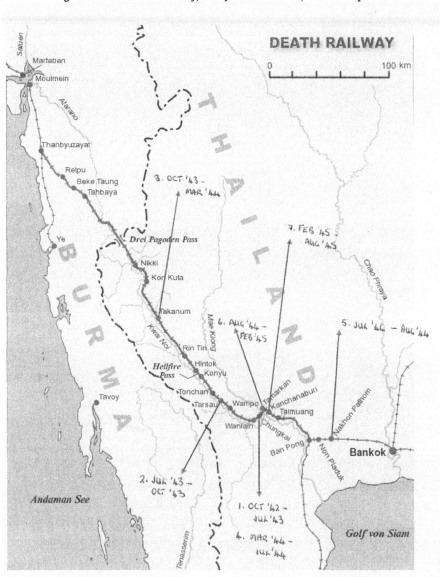

He stays here until July 1943, and it's worth painting a picture of what working on the Siam-Burma Railway involves. It has several different components:

Initially, collecting logs which have been floated downstream. This involves spending the day up to your neck in river water grabbing timber and pushing it to the shoreline so others can stack it at the water's edge for transport to sawmills. Here it will be fashioned into sleepers.

Then, clearing blasted sections of ground after charges had been laid and set off by Japanese engineers, using baskets suspended from poles to take the dirt and rubble away. Once the ground had been cleared and wood gathered, the slave labourers built embankments using primitive hand tools, often at great heights. Many years later, John can still only manage heights with great difficulty.

The POWs are organised in working parties and given a target to meet over a six-day period. In the early days, the targets are achievable in five or even four days, giving the soldiers one or two days off. Later, as completion deadlines loom, "Speedo" is introduced, targets are increased, and time off disappears. At its peak, work is going on for 16 hours a day.

Initially officers do not work, instead supervising work parties, or just sitting on their beds reading. And there are many British officers without men to command, since they are from Indian Army units which have been dissolved when the soldiers deserted en-masse. In December 1942, this practice comes to an end when the Japanese insist that they join the work parties. Here's what an American engineer thought:

"What makes this an engineering feat is the totality of it, the accumulation of factors. The total length (415 km), the total number of bridges- over 600, including six to eight long span bridges- the total number of people who were involved (one quarter of a million), the very short time in which they managed to accomplish it (one year)

and the extreme conditions they accomplished it under.
They had very little transportation to get stuff to and from
the workers, they had almost no medication, they couldn't
get food let alone materials, they had no tools to work with
except for basic things like spades and hammers, and they
worked in extremely difficult conditions - in the jungle
with its heat and humidity. All that, makes this railway
an extraordinary accomplishment."

(The Bridges of the Thai Burma Railway- PBS).

At this point in November 1942, John is 22, and has been away from Britain for just over a year, during which time he has been part of the most calamitous defeat in the British Army's history. He is part of a half-starved workforce building a railway by hand through thick virgin jungle in monsoon rains. As an officer, he is supervising work parties but will soon have to participate fully in their labours.

John and others are taking highly risky opportunities to sabotage their own work, for instance by pushing logs and brushwood into embankments to encourage later collapses. If they are caught, the mildest penalty is likely to be confinement for several days in an enclosure without room to stand or lie fully. Death by shooting or bayonet, having dug your own grave, is the penalty for escapes, and for keeping one of the secret radios which are in use from February 1943 onwards.

Tropical diseases such as cholera, beri-beri and dysentery profit from the insanitary conditions, and appropriate drugs are practically non-existent. Battalion funds, which have been brought up from Singapore, are supporting some of the sick with extra food and medicine but as the railway pushes up country, supplies peter out. The Red Cross, which has the job of looking after the welfare of prisoners of war and ensuring that they are being treated properly, is unable to extend much protection to the Railway POWs, located as they are miles away from roads or communications. Parcels of food, sent by neutral countries such as Sweden or Switzerland, do occasionally get through, but are mostly stolen by the Japanese Army or just kept back. Mail reaches the POWs infrequently and sparsely. During the whole period of his captivity a total of three post-cards from John reached Mig.

Fig 14 below: These cards cram as much information as John could manage into what he could send. The lists of names was meant to indicate that he had received the letters in which the people had been mentioned.

No 129954 LIEUT J.E.CROOKE

MY DEAR MAMMA,

JUST A LINE TO LET YOU KNOW I AM A PRISONER-OF-WAR, VERY FIT AND QUITE HAPPY. LONGING TO GET HOME AND SEE YOU ALL AGAIN. DON'T WORRY. TONS OF LOVE

John.

IMPERIAL JAPANESE ARMY

Date 22 JAN 1944

Your mails (and OTHERS) are received with thanks.
My health is (good, usual, poor).
I am ill in hospital.
I am working for pay (I am paid monthly salary).
I am not working.
My best regards to HUGH, PAT, GRANNIE, PHYLLIS, INJA, MARGARET, JOHN AND ELIZABETH, PETER AND PEGGY

Yours ever,

IMPERIAL JAPANESE ARMY

Date 22 MAY 1944.

ALSO RED X GIFTS
Your mails (and OTHERS) are received with thanks.
My health is (good, usual, poor).
I am ill in hospital.
I am working for pay (I am paid monthly salary).
I am not working.
My best regards to HUGH, PAT, GRANNIE, DICK, MOLLY, HÉLOÏSE, REGGIE, INJA, MILLY, MARGARET, FRANK, VERA, PHYLLIS, MATTHEW

Yours ever,

John.

By the spring of 1943, the tide of war is moving against the Japanese. Between June and October, the Japanese guards implement "Speedo", aimed at completing the railway, and providing them with a secure land-based supply route to the Assam front. First twelve, then sixteen, then 24-hour days are worked by the light of torches and with constant beatings and other punishments. In April 1943, the POWs complete a fully functioning railway bridge at the Wampo viaduct in three weeks, from scratch.

The authorities cut rations and hoard medicine stocks, and when the monsoon starts in May, the combination of exhaustion, filthy conditions and constant rain generating swarms of airborne insects results in a major cholera epidemic:

"Cholera first manifested itself in the camps for Asian labourers, where sanitary conditions were appalling. The POW doctors were highly alarmed and attempted to persuade the Japanese camp administrators to introduce strict hygiene control arrangements to prevent the spread of the disease to POW and Japanese camps. Their demands initially fell on deaf ears, with the Japanese believing that this was just another ruse to prevent men working on the line. They finally realised the extent of the danger when numbers of Japanese. succumbed to the disease, and half-heartedly began to cooperate with the POW doctors.

By then it was too late. Between May and October 1943 cholera quickly spread along the entire length of the line, and the best efforts of the POW doctors and camp officials were unable to stop it."
(The Thai-Burma Railway by Rod Beattie)

Over 60% of all Allied POW deaths on the railway happened during this time. Things were much worse on the Burma section than the Thai section- where death rates approached

30% at the epidemic's peak. The deaths nearly include John; he later tells of his life being saved by a live action blood transfusion from his comrades via a bamboo bucket into his veins using a bamboo cannula, which pulled him through.

Despite all this, by October 1943 the railway was finished. The two halves meet on 25 October, and the meeting is filmed with senior Japanese officers formally shaking hands with some of the more presentable POWS. Some senior British officers are entertained to lunch by their Japanese counterparts.

One cutting, nicknamed Hellfire Pass, 70 metres deep and 500 metres long, costs 700 lives to construct- one for each sleeper in the railway line.

Reflection: John, like most POWs, bitterly resented the picture painted by the film "Bridge over the River Kwai" of a bone headed officer played by Alec Guinness, forcing his men to build an enemy railway. The reality was that officers had to mediate between the demands of the Japanese engineers and Korean guards, and the exhaustion of their men. It is true that the railway, of which the bridge was part, was built in record time, but by exhausted, skeletal slaves, who nevertheless tried to sabotage it. And it is true that once the railway was complete, treatment improved.

CHAPTER 10

After the Railway

CHUNGKAI THEATRE
THAILAND

COMMENCING FRI. MAY. 19ᵗʰ 1944.
NIGHTLY 8.45 P.M

| GUS HARFFEY | DOUGLAS MORRIS |
| BOBBY SPONG | SAM FLICK |

THAILAND'S BIGGEST MUSICAL PLAY

WONDER BAR

REWRITTEN BY JOHN BECKETT
PRODUCED BY LEO BRITT

| JAMES CLARK | EDDIE EDWINS |

PAT DONOVAN	RENE DEN DAAS
DICK LUCAS	EDDIE MONKHOUSE
FRED THOMPSON	HUGH de WARDENER
EVERARD WOODS	DONALD GLANFIELD
HAROLD PYCOCK	GERALD ANGIER

| JOHN "NELLIE" WALLACE | SANDY MUNNOCH |

ERNEST LENTHALL AND HIS BAND

It is June 8th, 1944. The Camp theatre at Chungkai is heaving, Leo Britt and Bobby Spong are mounting one of their reviews, featuring them in a variety of women's outfits. When these had first appeared, the Japanese officers had been so captivated by their performances that they had insisted on checking the sexual credentials of the two men. Spong especially, seems to have been a stellar female impersonator. Tragically, he was killed when the ship he and hundreds of other POWs were being transported to Japan in, was sunk by a US submarine. He had carried 22 dresses with him in his kit.

Tonight, John Crooke is reciting a poem by Arthur Clough, "Say not the struggle nought availeth":

Say not the struggle nought availeth,
The labour and the wounds are vain,
The enemy faints not, nor faileth,
And as things have been they remain.

If hopes were dupes, fears may be liars;
It may be, in yon smoke concealed,
Your comrades chase e'en now the fliers,
And, but for you, possess the field.

For while the tired waves, vainly breaking
Seem here no painful inch to gain,
Far back through creeks and inlets making,
Comes silent, flooding in, the main.

And not by eastern windows only,
When daylight comes, comes in the light,
In front the sun climbs slow, how slowly,
But westward, look, the land is bright.

Say not the struggle nought availeth,
The labour and the wounds are in vain

The enemy faints not nor faileth,
And as things have been, they remain

The words in bold are lightly coded confirmation of the D-Day landings, which have taken place two days before, and reported on the secret radios which a few brave men are hiding. The theatre erupts in cheering and applause from the Allied POWs. The Japanese officers, who are little better-informed join in out of courtesy.

Now the Railway has been completed, it does its job of transporting men and supplies to the front in Assam. Whether it is because the railway has been built, or because the Japanese are increasingly aware that the war in the West is going against the Axis powers, treatment of the POWs improves somewhat.

The only major remaining engineering work is the construction of two bridges. One is bamboo, requiring the driving in of each pile by groups of POWs up to their waist in water. The other is made of concrete and steel, recovered from a railway bridge in Java. Suddenly, there is truly little for the POWs to do, except maintain the railway they have built. They are gradually shipped back down the line towards Banpong, the rail head. This allows those so inclined to give full vent to the English penchant for amateur dramatics, and we know that John is a keen thespian.

A theatre is built at Chungkai, the base camp and HQ for Group 2, and ambitious concerts and musicals are held there, attended by Japanese officers fascinated by cross dressing performers like Leo Britt and Bobby Spong. By this time, all trace of uniform has gone, and most men wear loincloths called Jap Happies. Bobby Spong's is pink.

The secret radios bravely guarded by some POWs get the news of D day in early June 1944.

In August 1944 John is sent to Tamarkan camp. Bombing raids by the USAAF on the railway line are becoming heavier as the Allies try to interdict the movement of Japanese supplies towards their Assam front. John is present at one raid which destroys POW living quarters near the rail line, burying nearly 80 prisoners. He is forced to stand on parade with other officers for hours, before being given permission to rescue them. 17 are killed and 60 are injured. Better treatment has its limits.

It's worth spending a little time trying to understand the nature of the Japanese Siam Burma Railway project. It was conceived as the way to ensure uninterrupted supplies of men and material to the battle front in Assam, on the Indian border with Burma, by avoiding the increasingly hazardous route through the Straits of Melaka, vulnerable to US submarines. There was a ready-made pool of labour available in the unexpectedly large numbers of Allied POWs, and inhabitants of the conquered territories who were deemed as hostile or unimportant (so not Malays or Thais, but Tamils, Burmese, and Indonesians). Anywhere from 200,000 to 500,000 Asian labourers from Malaya, Indonesia, and Burma, and 64000 Allied POWs were involved in building the Siam Burma Railway. 90,000 Asians and 12,300 POWs died. 69 Allied POWs were beaten to death, and unnumbered Asians. As horrific as the treatment of the POWs has been, it has been much worse for the Asian civilians; without any organisational or disciplinary imperative, red cross supplies or medicines, they have died in vast numbers. Using a British plan, which had been put aside as unachievable, and slave labour, the Japanese completed a functioning railway in a year, a stunning civil engineering project, even if it did cost the lives of over 100,000 slave labourers and Allied POWs.

The 64,000 POWs, half of them British, were guarded and administered by a Japanese POW Administration of about 130 Japanese officers and NCOs and 3000 conscripted Korean and Taiwanese guards. The Korean guards tended to be young, ill-educated men who had been provided by local Korean districts in response to a levy from their Japanese colonisers. Thrust into unwanted guard duties in the hostile jungle environment with minimal supervision, they tended to behave with great brutality. Language training did not form part of their induction, and sometimes they were in sole charge of the smaller camps. Leave young, ill-educated, armed men, who are themselves there against their will, in charge of powerless slaves, and the consequences are clear.

The Allied officers had the task of mediating the increasingly frantic demands of the Japanese engineers for greater and greater efforts, as well as trying to protect the sickest prisoners. These efforts varied hugely depending on the nature of the Korean guards and Japanese officers they had to deal with. Some were reasonable and even decent, but most were not, reflecting the brutal Japanese approach to military service, warfare, and surrender. They were particularly contemptuous of illness as an example of unacceptable physical frailty and made no provision at all for medical care. This was left entirely to the POWs to provide.

The British elements of the POWs on the Railway were extremely varied. The bulk were part of 18th Division, of which the Beds and Herts were part , but there were also many plantation and tin mine managers, as well as colonial civil servants who had enlisted in the volunteer military units. John would have spent much time with these men and used later to do an impression of them bemoaning the ending of the pre-war glory days for their kind ; "*Whisky a dollar a bottle, Gin 60 cents*". Still, they would have talked to him about their working lives, and perhaps he saved these thoughts for when the war ended, and he was back in the UK thinking about jobs.

The project's success, and the survival of the POWs depended on internal discipline and organisation being maintained via officers like John. They negotiated work targets, hours and rest days with the Japanese and Koreans and organised and managed canteen and hospital facilities once on the railway. The composition of the work parties sent up to Thailand from Singapore from September 1942 onwards was only specified by the Japanese in terms of numbers of men and officers, particularly limiting the latter. When sending parties, officers in Singapore tried to retain for as long as possible the nucleus of a fighting force in the form of front-line troops, should the opportunity arise, so those sent initially tended to be from support formations. So, units like the Beds and Herts found themselves split up, and it's probably also why John, as a signals officer was in one of the first parties to go. Because of the shortage of officers, he found himself in charge of up to hundreds of men, who relied on him to keep them safe and sound.

Everything was far worse for the Asian labourers. The Japanese authorities initially tried to fill their required totals of labourers by means of advertisements promising short contracts, good wages, and housing - all lies, but enough to attract some who even brought their wives. When they failed to attract the required numbers, they just rounded workers up from target communities, mostly Tamils, and packed them off to Thailand. One estimate calculates that the Tamil population of Malaya decreased by 7% during World War 2. These poor people lacked any of the organisation, supplies and funds enjoyed by the POWs, and as far as we can tell from the largely absent records, about half of them died There are many examples of the two slave communities helping each other, with British doctors working in the non-POW camps, and non-POWs helping POWs on and off trains, but this mutual aid was informal and haphazard, and had no great effect on the death toll.

Robert Hardie, a British POW doctor, wrote:

> "A lot of Tamil, Chinese and Malay labourers from Malaya have been brought up forcibly to work on the railway. They were told that they were going to Alor Star in northern Malaya; that conditions would be good - light work, good food and good quarters. Once on the train, however, they were kept under guard and brought right up to Siam and marched in droves up to the camps on the river. There must be many thousands of these unfortunates all along the railway course. There is a big camp a few kilometres below here, and another 2 or 3 kilometres up. We hear of the frightful casualties from cholera and other

diseases among these people and of the brutality with which they are treated by the Japanese. People who have been near the camps speak with bated breath of the state of affairs - corpses rotting unburied in the jungle, almost complete lack of sanitation, frightful stench, overcrowding, swarms of flies. There is no medical attention in these camps, and the wretched natives are of course unable to organise any communal sanitation...When one hears of these widespread barbarities, one can only feel that we prisoners of war, despite all the deaths and permanent disabilities which result, are being treated with comparative consideration."

When the railway was finished in October 1943, the POWs were brought back down the line towards Bangkok, but the Asians were left along the line to maintain it. They remained there until the end of the war, dying in large numbers. When the war was over, the Allies mounted a huge operation (Recovery of Allied Prisoners of War and Internees-RAPWI) to repatriate the civilian and military prisoners of the Japanese. Some efforts seemed to have been made to repatriate Asian workers, but to nowhere near the same extent as the POWs. Of the rest, some eventually made their way back home through the post war confusion, but many just stayed where they were.

Reflection: *It's clear that, despite the suffering John and his comrades went through, the Asian railway labourers had a far worse time of it, both in terms of numbers involved and mortality rates. Lacking the organisational structure and resources (limited as they were) which were available to the Allied POWs, the Asians died in droves. And when it was all over, the Allied authorities expended far less effort to bring them home.*

Fig 16: Memorial remembering both Allied POWs and Asian slave labourers erected in front of Ipoh station, Malaysia

CHAPTER 11

The End of the War?

A band of 400 skeletal prisoners of war, including John, are staggering down a laterite road in the searing midday heat of Thailand, towards a newly created camp for officers at Nakhon Nayok, near Bangkok.

Four days earlier, an atomic bomb has exploded over Hiroshima, and a second hit Nagasaki yesterday. Shortly, Emperor Hirohito will broadcast to his people. The words defeat and surrender will not be mentioned. Instead, he will employ the massive understatement that "the war situation having developed not necessarily to Japan's advantage" it would be best to stop fighting.

In a quite massive irony, the first part of the prisoners' journey is made by train on the railway tracks they have built.

That stops when they come to a bombed railway bridge. Then they must march in single file, at 20-yard intervals across the bridge. John is carrying a 55 lb pack and some kit for others who are too weak to do it for themselves.

Bamboos have been laid loosely across the gap and a single wire is strung at or above head height. 50 foot below is the raging torrent of a rain swollen river. Crossing this gap with over 70 lbs of kit is one of the most terrifying things John has ever had to do, and he is haunted by it for the rest of his life.
Somehow, everybody makes it across...

August 1945. The road shimmers in the intense mid-day heat of Thailand. John and a group of 400 half-starved British, Australian, and Dutch officers are marching down it to a new camp for officers at the little settlement of Nakhon Nayok, east of Bangkok. They left their previous camp at Kanchanaburi on 10 August, four days after the Hiroshima atomic bomb explodes and the day after the second bomb at Nagasaki, but know nothing about it. John later writes an account of this time for broadcast on the BBC on the second anniversary of the end of the war. It is quoted from here.

It seems clear now that the new camp was intended to assemble officers as hostages for execution. Even before the bombs, the war is heading for defeat for Japan, and those responsible for the railway camps and their attendant atrocities will want as few witnesses as possible to their deeds. As far as John is concerned, it is the latest of nine different camps he has been in since the British surrender in February 1942.

In a supreme irony, the first part of this journey has been in steel trucks on the railway that he and his comrades have built. Then the train stops, and they must cross a partially destroyed railway bridge. John will remember this ordeal until his own end. He is never able to manage heights again.

Along the route, John sees Thais flashing V for Victory signs to them, and gradually it dawns on him that the war might finally be over. When Captain Noguchi, their Japanese commander, signals them to sit down after his inspection on 15th August, the POWs know something is up. Noguchi has been a brutal and sadistic commander who would never do such a thing in normal circumstances.

Nevertheless, the march goes on down an endless red laterite road. John's kit weighs 55 1bs, about two thirds of his then body weight, and digs into what's left of his flesh. He's also taking his turn carrying the kit of men too weak to carry their own, and the loose communal cooking gear. In traditional British Army route march style, they stop once an hour for 10 minutes, and when this happens near a stream, the prohibition on drinking un-boiled water, which they have kept to for the last 3 ½ years, is abandoned and they drink deeply.

By this stage, they are being fed by lorries coming from

their new camp, and rumours of something big happening are being shared.

By this time John is near the end of his tether.

> *"My steps wandered; I was like a drunk man, with no control over my feet. My breath was coming out in peculiar little moans at each step. I had to keep my eyes fixed on the ground a few paces ahead. My head swam and my equipment bit into my flesh."*

Somehow, he keeps going, and a mile away from camp they come across fellow POWs who had arrived earlier and are finishing a day's bamboo cutting.

> *"Johnny, mate. You look like shit! You'll ruin that kit you're carrying sweating like that. Go on, I'll take it".*

> *"No, mate, I'm fine, nothing to it."*

A ridiculous wrestling match between two skeletons ensues, and John is eventually relieved of half his load. Thus, he staggers into camp to find the residents at fever pitch. They are addressed by Lt Col Toosey, an inspirational commander in the camps, and a model for the obsessive character played by Alec Guinness in Bridge over the River Kwai.

> *"Men, I believe that the Japanese may have surrendered, and intend to confront Captain Noguchi about it. Remain as you are until I have definite news. There are to be no reprisals".*

The concern must be that the Japanese troops will implement the plan to shoot the POW's.

The following morning (16th August, nearly a week after the Nagasaki bomb) Col Toosey marches into Noguchi's office.

John's account of the conversation;

"Captain Noguchi, I know that Japan has surrendered. You are to surrender control of this camp to me as the Senior British Officer. You and your men will not be harmed, but are now under my command"

"Yes, it is so. The war is over, and I hope that we can now be friends".

The news spreads like wildfire.

"Everyone swarmed out of the huts; Union Jacks and other Allied flags appeared as by magic and were run up on long bamboos. As darkness fell, we began to sing. Our national anthems rolled forth and echoed against the surrounding hills; our souls were in our songs, and in our hearts was hope. Those of us who were still alive thanked God. WE, at least, had truly learned the value of Freedom."

CHAPTER 12

Homeward Bound

John and fellow officers from the Beds and Herts are with a hundred or so other officers in the garrison cinema of the Rangoon Naval Base. It is three weeks after they arrived in the city by DC3 aircraft from Thailand, and they are all noticeably less skinny. They have been very well treated by the RAPWI (Repatriation of Allied POWs and Internees) organisation, with new clothing, including tailored uniforms, full medicals, haircuts, and manicures. They note however, that the "cost" of their accommodation while in prison camp has been deducted from their back pay for the period of their imprisonment.

The local British military community has entertained them royally, showing them the sights and wining and dining them to such an extent that their shrunken stomachs have rebelled. Now they want to go home, and they are hoping that their visitor will tell them when.

A door at the back of the room opens and a handsome man in the white tropical dress uniform of an Admiral of the Fleet sweeps in.

He is Lord Louis Mountbatten, Supreme Allied Commander South East Asia. The entire left-hand side of his chest is covered with medal ribbons, and John remembers later wondering how Mountbatten could have got them all when he only has three (the answer is that it helps to be related to most of the royal houses in Europe and to have had a destroyer sunk under you). The brave men who hid secret radios for three years will get nothing.

John and his fellow officers stand to attention.

"At ease, chaps" drawls Mountbatten. "come to see how you are. We

treating you well?" There is a muttered affirmative. "Well, look, I know you want to go home, and you will, soon. Got a bit of bother with shipping - everybody seems to want to go home at the same time. So, hang fire for another week or so, and we'll get you on your way". Ignoring the groans of disappointment, Mountbatten sweeps out. Eighteen months later he would be dismembering India

Despite the brutality of the previous three years, there are no reprisals against the Japanese and Korean guards after the surrender. Piles of Red Cross parcels appear from the storage they had been kept in, shortly followed by paratroopers and soldiers from Force 136, the stay-behind British force which had hidden in the jungles of Malaya and Thailand.

The remarkable thing about the next few days and weeks in Thailand is this almost completely orderly nature of the transition from Japanese control and dominance. There seems to be little appetite from the POW's for revenge, and this is encouraged by the rapid assumption of control over the camps by the airdropped paras and Force 136. They rapidly switch the focus of their operation, from military defeat of the Japanese and rescue of the POWs, to supplying feeding, clothing, and medical needs, then transporting them out of the jungle.

These needs border on the overwhelming. John is probably typical in having lost half his bodyweight, and survived cholera, dysentery, and tropical ulcers. Although Japan surrenders unconditionally on 14 August, it is the end of August 1945 before all Japanese units have surrendered, so initially the POWs are kept where they are. During September, the POWs are flown in groups of 25 by Dakota (DC 3) transport aircraft to Rangoon and Singapore. The 5th Beds and Herts stay here for over a month. Lord Louis Mountbatten, Supreme Allied Commander for South East Asia, and relative of the British King, visits them to explain that logistical problems are responsible, but John's own view is that they are being kept out of sight until they look a bit less frighteningly thin. They are also advised not to go on about their war experiences, because nobody will be interested. It is after all three months since the end of the war in Europe; there is a new (Labour) Prime Minister and a Welfare State. People want to look forward, not back. So, keep it to yourself, they said, and John and his comrades largely did, to the medium - and long-term detriment of their physical and mental health.

Eventually, it was the 5th Beds and Herts' turn to board ship in Rangoon for home, almost exactly four years after they left. In November 1945, their ship docks at Liverpool.

Family memories clash as to the nature of John's reunion with his mother and brothers. By this time, Hugh had enlisted in the RAF, been trained as a navigator in India and was now awaiting demobilization himself. Pat was about to join the army for his national service but would also be a civilian again within months.

Pat remembers Mig being lent a car by a wealthy friend (the middle class mafia again) and being driven up to Liverpool to meet him. Hugh remembers him *"coming back to Euston by train and my being taken by car to meet him.... Mig couldn't face a possible scene; the bottled-up wretchedness would perhaps have exploded, and she wanted to welcome him at home, not in a public place. At least so I guess"*.

Both brothers remember a little ceremony in the back garden of their house, in which John lays out the belongings he had carried through his experience; a rusty razor, a jap happy, a comb and a bit of tobacco, and consigns them to the past with the support of his family. John says *"I suppose I won't be needing these anymore"*

Reflection: Knowing what we now know about the long-term effect of the traumatic events he has been through, this seems like a noble wish rather than actual fact, but it certainly marks the point where John's life begins again.

PART TWO

CHAPTER 13

Happy Christmas, War is Over

The Hood Arms in East Quantoxhead is a cosy pub on the edge of Exmoor in North Somerset. In this, the first summer after the war, business is quite brisk despite rationing, which restricts the amount and variety of food available. Beer is plentiful though and most evenings the public bar is full of local farmers and labourers.

John and Mary prefer the snug, which they can generally have to themselves. Their days are spent walking the glorious countryside and swimming in the beaches and coves, and this evening they are both tanned and relaxed. John tries not to think too hard of the fact that this time a year ago he was frantically digging through the wreckage of bamboo huts destroyed by American bombers.

He is now sleeping much better than when he first returned, but still finds it difficult to explain to Mary what he has been through. It's been made clear to him and the other returning POWs that they are to get on with things, and not make a fuss. He still has the deep tan from the years of outside work in Thailand, and occasionally someone will ask him about it, but once he explains that he was on the Death Railway, as it is known, people's attention generally drifts away.

He knows, though, that he must get away from the Medical Sickness Annuity Society Ltd, his pre-war job which has been kept for him. The tedium of insurance underwriting after what he went through is, he is finding, unbearable. Tin mines and rubber estates in the Malay States are being re-opened and young men like him, recruited to run them. John recalls conversations in prison camp with fellow planter captives about the life. Mary finds it hard to under-

stand why he would want to go back there but can see that he is unhappy; she has heard enough about his experiences to understand that he might want to face his demons in this way. She is qualifying as a social worker at the LSE, but as women were expected to then, she subordinates her career to his.

By the time the honeymoon finishes, it is decided. John will apply for a position as an Assistant Manager on a rubber estate....

In the prosperous Hertfordshire market town of Berkhamsted, the weather for the first peacetime Christmas for six years is unseasonably mild, and damp. Celebrations are hampered slightly by the extreme rationing not only still in force, but more severe than in the last months of war. The food ration allows tiny quantities of meat and dairy products, and no slack is cut for Christmas. A turkey is out of the question, but would probably have been so pre-war as well, however, some try to create a pretend version of hoarded sausage meat and breadcrumbs. Even paper is in short supply, so paperchains are made of painted newspaper, which also serves to wrap meagre presents. Cinemas offer an escape, and are packed, with some even opening on the evening of Christmas Day. Bing Crosby's White Christmas remains a firm favourite.

Nevertheless, the streets are full of people, older civilians, and younger men and women recently demobilized from the wartime armed forces. Two should get our attention. They are part of the local church's carol singing group. One is Lucy, always called Mary, Pagden who is 24, and has lived round the corner from the other, John Crooke, all her life. They barely know each other, despite apparently having played together once when they were exceedingly small.

Mary's family has a not dissimilar middle class and colonial background to John's, but her father has had to leave his job in the Colonial Service in East Africa through ill health, and since the mid-1930s he, and his family, have depended on sinecure jobs and largesse from the related Cooper family, made wealthy by Cooper's Sheep Dip. Mary knows her father is a dissatisfied man. Her two elder brothers have received the lion's share of the family resources, and Mary, unkindly nicknamed "Podge", has grown up feeling inadequate and inferior. In her "interview with Grandma", granted to 14-year-old Tom and 11-year-old Daisy in October 2004 (attached as Appendix 2), she relates how she had to leave school after the equivalent of O levels because her parents "had three other children to educate".

There were only two scholarships available in the county for girls. When war broke out Mary was working in a private nursery school run by a pair of middle-aged ladies, which was later immortalised in a series of children's books featuring a boy hero called Bobby Brewster. Mary recalls that everybody around her was joining up, and girls of her class were heavily encouraged to join the Women's Royal Naval Service (WRENs) or the First Aid Nursing Yeomanry (FANYs). In what might have been her first act of defiance, she decided to apply to the Women's Auxiliary Air Force, and on the second time of asking, she got in.

Fig 17: Mary pictured around the time of joining the WAAF

Mary served in the WAAF in the early part of the war. During the Battle of Britain her job was, under threat of aerial attack, to move models of enemy and RAF aircraft squadrons around large scale maps in deep shelters for the commanders deploying stretched resources.

Family legend, confirmed by Mary in her interview, has

it that on one occasion she was asked to make tea for Winston Churchill during one of the PM's visits, which in her nervousness, she managed to do without using any actual tea. After the Battle of Britain, and before her discharge with health problems, she also packed some new tin legs to be parachuted into Germany by the Red Cross for Group Captain Douglas Bader, a legless fighter ace Prisoner of War who had bailed out of his Spitfire without his previous set of lower limbs. She was commissioned as an officer and despite then being invalided out, the whole experience seems to have given her some much-needed self-confidence. She is now studying for a Social Work diploma at the London School of Economics.

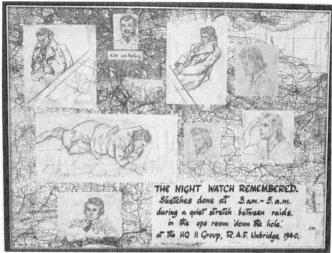

Fig 18: Collage by Mary's friend Kyttern depicting life in the RAF Uxbridge Ops Room during the Battle of Britain. Mary is at bottom left.

Mary and John both have fine singing voices, and share a love of singing, along with enthusiasm for amateur dramatics, and strong Anglican religious faith. Mary had become engaged in 1943 to Derek Horne, a Captain in the Black Watch highland regiment, who was killed near Caen in late 1944. John too had had a romantic attachment before the war, which seems to have stayed alive after his return, but by early 1946, they are, in modern parlance, an item, and John later recounts his painful trip to end the relationship with his ex:

X had written to me throughout the war, although I had never got one of her letters. We had both changed from the naïve young things we were when we met, and in my case, I had to accept that meant I did not now love her in the way I might have done then- even without the experience of Prison Camp. She lived on a farm in Scotland and I travelled there after Christmas. We talked about ourselves, each other and my experiences in Thailand and parted as friends. Quite soon afterwards, she announced her engagement to a local farmer, married him and had children.

Like most wartime soldiers who had left permanent jobs to join up, John has returned to his post as a clerk for the Medical Sickness Society. He is finding this job less than gripping and has already sought employment abroad with the Colonial Office. Although this is unsuccessful, it seems that John is determined to return to South East Asia, the region where he has suffered his greatest trial.

In the meantime, this young couple have been brought together by their common interests and intense wartime experiences in a post-war society which combines shortages and deprivations with great social upheavals and hopes for the future.

They marry in July 1946. Mary's father had died in 1940, and the wedding is organised and sponsored by the wealthy benefactors on each side, Reggie and Heloise Martin for John, and Frank Cooper on Mary's behalf. Rationing ensures a generally modest tone, but we can take it that the celebrations would not have lacked resources. They take place at a grand house in Hertfordshire, and Mary and John spend their honeymoon staying in a country pub in North Somerset. They have the use of a small car and they seem to have spent their time exploring the Quantocks, walking, and swimming.

Their drives, walks and swims give them time to get to know each other and understand perhaps how they have both come to this point in their lives. For Mary it has meant over-coming the obstacles in her way as a woman and an overlooked daughter to serve in the WAAF with distinction, and gain admission to the London School of Economics. For John, it is the early loss of his father and assumption of family responsibilities, his war service, and hellish experiences as a prisoner of war on the other side of the world.

After the big wedding and modest honeymoon, Mary's and John's early married life is spent in a small, rented flat in Notting Hill Gate. John is still at the Medical Sickness Society and Mary qualifies from the LSE as a hospital almoner- what would now be known as a medical social worker. Although her marriage to John and move to South East Asia to be with him means that she hardly practiced her original profession, she remains justifiably immensely proud of her achievement until the end of her life. She is typical of thousands of women who entered caring professions and will herself start a nursery school and later teach, while carrying out what some would have said was her main role of wife and mother.

Reflection: The more I find out about Mary's early life, the more I am humbled by her courage and tenacity. In her interview with Tom and Daisy (Appendix 2), she talks about crying herself to sleep with homesickness when she joins the WAAF, and we can imagine that she did the same when she first arrived in Malaya, but in both huge undertakings she overcame the obstacles in her way. She showed grit again when she insisted on a return to the UK at a time when it might have been possible for John to get another rubber industry job. I can also understand what it must have cost her to lose us to boarding school in Penang and then the UK, even as I despair at the thinking which forced her to do it.

As for John's perhaps baffling decision to return to South East Asia; The Medical Sickness Annuity Society job that he had come back to must have seemed unutterably tedious to him after his wartime experiences, and we know that the rubber industry was seeking men of exactly his type; some knowledge of the area, proven resili-

ence, and military experience to restart the industry in dangerous, isolated circumstances. And we must remember that the Britain of the time was still a worldwide imperial power, where it would have been quite normal for young men to travel halfway round the world to work in some aspect of the imperial project. As importantly, it would have been assumed that the fiancé or wife of such a man would, eventually join him in his far-flung outpost of Empire and manage his home life. Finally, John's appetite for a career in rubber plantations may well have been whetted by fellow POWs. Somehow, he must have made it clear to Mary that he had to go back to that place, and that he wanted her to come with him. And she must have understood.

CHAPTER 14

Sungei Toh Pawang

Sungei Toh Pawang Rubber Estate, Early 1949. Mary is doing what she does most of the time, writing letters home. She has been in Malaya for three months, and is desperately, paralyzingly home-sick. John is kind and understanding but is either out on the estate in varying degrees of danger or in the office most of the day. Their social life revolves round the two clubs they belong to: Harvard swimming and golf club, and Sungei Patani golf and tennis club, with the wives playing Bridge and tennis, interspersed by coffee mornings. Mary's tennis is good (she will later become the mixed doubles champion of Kedah State) but Bridge is eluding her. Later, people in her position will be given induction and language training, but she and those like her are expected just to get on with it.

John is the most junior of three assistant managers, and she is therefore the most junior wife. The manager's wife has, without asking her, organised the recruitment of Mary's domestic staff using her highly limited grasp of Tamil and Malay. Mary is trying to learn these languages but is still unable to understand the people being sent up to her house to be interviewed. The last of these has just left without anything being resolved.

Mary is quite close to tears when a small, slight Tamil woman arrives at the door, takes her sandals off, and slips into the large, airy living room.

For some reason, Mary and Devi understand each other straight away. Mary is able to tell Devi how helpless, frightened and lonely she feels, while Devi quietly, yet insistently, outlines the ways in which Mary might get control of the reins of the household and how Devi can help her.

It is at this point that there is wordless agreement between them that Devi will become Amah to the household, and her husband, Veloo, will be John's driver.

References may have been offered, but as I understand it Devi was informing Mary of a fact, rather than asking for a job. And that was that.

Fig 19: Foreground l to r - Roland, Ravi encouraging Celia to walk, Devi ready to step in while Mary watches anxiously. Background - Ramu off to burn the toast!

I'm sure that the extensive middle class network we have seen in operation already would have generated several opportunities, but the one John plumps for is at the Sungei Toh Pawang (STP) rubber estate, in Kedah. Kedah is a largely Malay state in the North West of the Malay peninsula. It is owned by the Eastern Industries plantation group(EI), quoted on the London stock exchange, and headquartered in the UK. EI is one of a number of expatriate companies, Dutch, British, French, Italian and United States owned with plantations in British Malaya. These estates have all ceased production during the Japanese occupation and have suffered damage to their infrastructure, not to mention their workforces, who have been scattered and left without work.

I imagine that there are many young men like John who find the tedium of daily working life in the UK with its cold, rationing and drab daily existence, hard to deal with. Many are likely to be with him when, on 28 October 1947 he sails from Liverpool on the 5-week voyage to Penang. He is 27 and has been married to Mary for just over a year.

The Malaya he arrives in in November 1947 is struggling to recover its economic and political equilibrium. Unlike Indonesia, on the other side of the Straits of Malacca, the British colonial authorities have managed to reassert some sort of control. An attempt to introduce a new political framework giving equal citizenship rights to Indian and Chinese peoples is speedily dropped when it is strongly opposed by the newly politicized Malays. Of the three main racial groups in Malaya/Malaysia, the Malays regard themselves as the original possessors of the land and were treated as the predominant race politically both by the British and the Japanese. The Malayan Union citizenship proposals described here are an attempt by the British to compensate for the earlier bad treatment of the Indians and Chinese by them and the Japanese. The Malays have developed political muscle during the Japanese occupation and use it to stop the proposals. They have after all witnessed the complete defeat and humiliation of their colonial masters not 5 years ago.

The wider world is rapidly becoming immersed in what Churchill christens the Cold War, and decolonisation is gathering pace in South East Asia as in Africa. India and Pakistan gain independence in 1947, with an accompanying bloodbath, and Burma becomes independent in 1948. In Malaya and the Borneo Territories, Britain maintains control, but desperately needs the resumption of supplies of tin and rubber to feed its own shattered and indebted economy – while the Malayan economy itself is on its knees after 3-4 years of war.

The Malayan Peoples Anti-Japanese Army has formally disbanded itself in December 1945, but the Malayan Communist Party continues to operate openly, with a strong presence in the nascent Trade Unions and the Chinese medium schools. It organises a 24-hour general strike in 1946 and a further 300 strikes in 1947. But its membership and support never broaden out much into the Indian and especially Malay communities. The Malay ruling structures are being reinforced and co-opted by the colonial authorities and remain antipathetic to the communist message.

So here is John the former insurance clerk, spending Christmas 1947 not far from the railway line that had taken him in a cattle truck to Thailand 5 years earlier. He is part of an expatriate community of plantation and tin mine managers, police officers, army officers and others. We know he belongs to two local clubs, one in the nearest town of Sungei Patani, and the other on the American owned Harvard estate adjoining STP which has a swimming pool and golf course (I am proud to say that he hated golf). He also at some point joins two further clubs in Penang; the Penang Club and the Penang Swimming Club, which has a spectacular saltwater pool built into the cliffs off the main round island road. These clubs still thrive in post-colonial Malaysia, but at the time would probably only be open to senior expats and local members of royalty and the governing structures. Importantly for John, the Sungei Patani club is home to an amateur dramatic club.

He also belongs to the local Anglican Church. His local place of worship is the church of St Philip and St James in the British army garrison in Sungei Patani, catering for expats and a growing number of Indian and Chinese Christians. He has a fine bass voice, and he becomes a leading light in the church. Later he will start and lead a church choir which his children will be expected to join on their summer holidays. His faith has somehow survived the deprivations of the war.

For the first 6 months of his working life in Malaya there is an uneasy peace in and around the estate. The daily routine of his working life involves supervising the replanting of the estate with rubber trees and managing the collection of latex from existing trees once they have been brought back into production. The work force he supervises is almost entirely Tamil, indentured labourers who have migrated from Southern India, and to communicate he must learn a basic version of their language, as well as Malay.

So early 1948 sees John, married but living a bachelor life many thousands of miles apart from his young wife, working hard in the open air and with a varied social life revolving around his clubs and the church.

Everything changes in June 1948. A former MPAJA commander called Chin Peng, who takes control of the MCP in 1947, sees that political change of the sort the MCP want is becoming increasingly unlikely, and is encouraged by the success of Mao Dzedong in China, to launch a military campaign against the colonial structures.

The start of the "Emergency" (so called to avoid the insurance premium implications of the word "war") is generally reckoned to be the killing of three English plantation managers on the Sungei Siput Estate in Perak state in June 1948. The MPAJA is reborn as the Malayan Peoples anti-British Army, and then the Malayan Races Liberation Army and the MCP is banned and goes underground.

The Emergency gives rise to a whole vocabulary; MRLA fighters are known as "CTs" (Communist Terrorists) or "bandits". A largely Malay auxiliary police force is raised, and its members are "SCs"(Special Constables).

John and other European planters are a prime target for the MRLA. Relatively isolated from each other on large estates, and far from centres of population, they depend on their workforces and on the security forces intelligence networks to give early warning of "bandit" presence in their areas. When the emergency starts, John has been back in Malaya for little more than 6 months. The security force presence is completely inadequate to provide close protection for him and the other isolated Europeans, and he must be very frightened on his own in his bungalow, despite the social life and support network that is in place.

In his favour is the fact that his estate is in Kedah, with its large Malay indigenous population, and has an almost entirely Tamil workforce. It is not one of the most favourable states for the largely Chinese guerrillas to operate in (Negeri Sembilan, Perak and Selangor are more so) because they depend largely on the peripheral Chinese squatter community to be supplied and supported. The support organisation is called the Minh Yuen or People's Organisation, and draws its strength from Chinese smallholders, tin miners, and vegetable growers without strong title to their land. A key part of the British led strategy for defeating the MRLA is the confinement of the Chinese rural population in "New Villages" to which they must return overnight. Food supplies are tightly controlled, with permits being issued to those licensed to buy and store food. Later, Mary will be charged with contravention of this regulation by a policewoman, quite rightly, because her permit was a week out of date. This embarrassment took quite a bit of sorting out with and by the authorities, especially as Mary was by then chairman of the local juvenile magistrates' bench.

Nevertheless, these early years of the Emergency sees British control in Malaya threatened as it has never been before.

In September 1948, Mary Crooke sails from Britain to join her husband in this highly dangerous environment. She is 27 and has never left Britain. She is coming to a place on the other side of the world in the grip of a civil war, where she will be expected to make and manage a home for her husband not knowing whether either or both might be killed at any minute.

The only reliable means of communication with the UK is by letter, either surface mail, which takes 4-5 weeks or airmail which takes 4-5 days, but whose cost means that only thin, flimsy letters are possible. Travel between the UK and Malaya is by passenger liner via the Suez Canal and India, or round the Cape of Good Hope and takes at least 4 weeks. Air travel is in its infancy and still takes several days at huge cost. Phone calls are possible but must be booked days in advance and are often unintelligible. Really urgent news goes by telegram, briefly, because you are charged by the word.

So, it is a bit like going to Mars - or off the end of the world, away from everything she knows. In the previous months she has lost a baby to miscarriage and is to do so twice more before I am born in 1951 - an event for which they return to the UK. John and Mary have been apart for a year, and Mary is frightened that she will not recognise her husband.

The experience I'm describing seems utterly alien to us today but is completely usual at that time. Expatriate households like John and Mary's would be supported by a small army of servants and a network of other Europeans, albeit widely scattered. In Mary's case, she is adopted by a small Tamil woman called Devi. Family legend (see Chapter 14) has it that Devi, walked into the house sometime in 1949 and told Mary that she (Devi) was going to start working for her because she had heard that Mary was not coping.

Fig 20: Devi, my other Mother, with me aged 2.

Some of my earliest and most treasured memories are of Devi in her floating sari effortlessly caring for us. As often happened, Devi comes with a husband who becomes our driver, and they live in the servants' quarters behind our house. Soon they are joined by a family of four children, , the eldest son Pany, daughters Santha and Vasantha, and Ravi aka Tambi (little brother in Tamil). They become in effect my brothers and sisters and in our early years we spend as much time with them as we do with our parents. Tambi, who is a year older than me being my playmate and constant companion. I would go around to the servants' quarters when I awoke, often for a Tamil breakfast of conjee porridge or puthu, a steamed mix of rice, coconut, and sugar, before being called back for the western version. By the time I was 4 my preferred language was Tamil.

Fig 21: My Tamil brother and sisters (l to r - Roland, Ravi, Santha, Celia and Vasantha looking as if they are about to face a firing squad!)

Looking back, I marvel at my Tamil family's forbearance. I would, despite the mild protestations of my mother, rush round there in the heat of the afternoon, when most people were resting, or in the early evening when they were washing or eating and I was always welcomed and included in what was going on. Tamils are Hindus. Their lives and quarters were strangely alien to me, and the two girls especially seemed mysteriously beautiful, with their dark skin and long black hair oiled with coconut. Devi's family worshipped the range of Hindu gods and goddesses, whose portraits and statues were everywhere in their rooms, often garlanded with frangipane flowers. They also observed the Hindu festivals, especially Deepavali and Thaipusam. For the latter, Tamil males are expected to show their devotion either by wearing Kavadis, metal structures anchored by hooks in their flesh, while parading down the street, or by walking across long beds of glowing coals in their bare feet. Veloo never seemed to manage to get himself into the right trance like state to allow him to do the latter without hobbling around in complete agony the next day.

Our domestic staff team was completed by Ramu, who, like Devi marched up to the house and offered his services as cook, though he was at that point, a rubber tapper. We loved Ramu nearly as much as Devi. He was an excellent cook, but a bit forgetful, and I grew up believing that burning toast was an essential part of making it. Ramu was putty in our hands; we could reduce him easily to a fit of helpless giggles, and if making a cake, he would shamelessly leave us half the bowl of mixture to gobble up. Ramu's elder son Krishnan became a medic in the fledgling Malaysian Army after 1962 and was promoted for service in Sarawak.

Fig 22: Ramu - waiting for the toast to burn

The other members of the team were the gardeners Maniam and Sinayah. The garden was Mary's territory, but she relied heavily on Maniam's advice. When we moved to our second house in 1964, on the sale of the original one, he persuaded her not to try to recreate an English garden. Instead, it was terraced with the lower level bordered by a fast-flowing muddy brown river. The area was quickly colonised by a troupe of "Kra" monkeys who hurled themselves from branch to branch in the trees bordering the river, chattering with hostility if they caught sight of us.

So, by the end of 1949, John and Mary's household in Malaya is established, albeit in low level civil war conditions. It is just over 4 years since the end of the war which consigned John to the hell of the Siam- Burma railway, and Mary to military service as a member of the Women's Auxiliary Air Force in the Battle of Britain. Now they have started one of many colonial households which will serve the British Empire in its final phase, and John's story will become intertwined with that of his family and the other members of that household.

Mary feels the pressure of this way of life more than John. She has, by 1953, two young children, after much difficulty and unsuccessful pregnancies. Roland, born in June 1951 and Celia born two years later. She has the formidable help of Devi in running the household, but certainly, during the early 50s is bringing them up in a war zone. She sees her husband, the father of her children, go out every day with a revolver strapped to his hip and with two armed guards. They have steel plates nailed to their bedroom walls and more armed guards in the garden. She only communicates with her family in the UK and elsewhere in the Empire by airmail letter and she has her own pistol to fire if necessary. Despite this, she starts and runs a nursery school, and becomes a juvenile bench magistrate.

CHAPTER 15

A Colonial Life

Roland wakes as usual to the sound of cicadas, murmured conversation from the kebuns and the smell of burning toast from Ramu's kitchen. At 6, he is looked after in the mornings, not by his mother but by Devi, who washes and dresses him in crisply ironed shirt and shorts. There had been some talk recently of going to somewhere called boarding school, but he takes no notice of it and runs round to the servants' quarters to see what Tambi is up to.

They are in the middle of a complicated game of mock battles, when the cattle grid at the end of the drive rattles under Daddy's Gipsy, and Roland is called back for breakfast. Daddy has completed his early inspection of the estate, and he, Veloo and the two SCs clamber out. Daddy unbuckles his gun belt and loops it over the screen at the back of the house's living area.

Roland loves this time of day; it's still quite cool, and Ramu, clad in white shirt, sarong and bare feet, offers Celia and him bacon and eggs from a large oval platter, discreetly pushing the crispiest pieces of bacon his way. He notices how Mummy cuts her burnt toast along the diagonal, spreads butter on both halves, and ensures it has all been incorporated by cleaning the knife in the inside of the toast. This is a hangover from rationing, when the butter ration had to be eked out by any means possible. The marmalade is similarly eked by being placed on the edge of the plate and added in small amounts to mouthfuls of toast.

But today his parents have something to tell him, and a sinking feeling consumes him. "Roland, darling", begins his mother. Now he knows something bad is coming- the last time she called him that was when his father had just smacked him with a hairbrush for the first and only time in his life.

For the first half of the 50s, the Crooke family life proceeded along lines which would be familiar to most, despite the semi-militarised conditions under which it lived. John and Mary both had personal handguns, Mary tried to remember to take hers with her when in the garden, and John always wore his when away from the house. A detachment of Malay special constables guarded the house, and the house's interior walls were lined with steel panels. Security operations would occasionally sweep through the estate, with Land Rovers, indigenous trackers from Borneo and tracker dogs on the trail of "CTs". I was once taken to the site of a contact with CTs and shown some leaves with rust-coloured stains. This was allegedly blood from an ambush set by the security forces.

I can still recall this time. Life for Celia and I alternated between sessions at the nursery school run by Mary in the house, visits to the servants' quarters, swimming sessions at Harvard swimming club and shopping in Sungei Patani and Penang. I played in the sun with Tambi and Celia, utterly safe and happy, and felt as if it would never end. Curiously, this time was also marked by a horrendous series of accidents. In one, I gashed my right leg on some carelessly placed barbed wire; in another I broke my arm falling from a climbing frame at the Sungei Patani Club, and in a third a playmate dropped a lead plumb line on my head, for reasons which now escape me. It must have seemed to John and Mary as if I had a death wish. The accidents continued at Uplands; I ran down some steps and swung round the newel post at the bottom, let go and smacked my face into the concrete. If I wasn't self-harming, I was setting at naught John and Mary's dental expenditure by hurling a teeth brace into the jungle on the way back up to school on the hill railway..... The two families in the house lived very closely together, and were intimate witnesses to each other's lives, but those lives were still separate in many respects, in terms of culture and standards of living. Domestic staff-work for the white Mems and Tuans was highly sought after and those doing it constituted an elite of sorts, but they were almost never going to join that society. It was not uncommon for a white Tuan to take an ayah or ayah's daughter as a mistress, particularly if his Mem was away, and there were occasional interracial marriages, but lives remained, overall, socially separate. This was the case across all communities in Malaya, they remained unmixed to any extent. This had not always been the case, early waves of Chinese immigrants, all males, formed relationships with Malay women which developed into its own discrete community; the Babas and Nyonyas.

Expatriate staff like John were entitled to three or four months "Home" leave every three or four years. The first of these in my life was in 1955, and now I see it as starting the process of distancing me from my Tamil family. I returned no longer able to speak the language and found that Tambi/Ravi had started school locally so was no longer always available as a playmate.

Thus, involuntarily, my path to adulthood started to diverge from that of Ravi and his siblings. Ravi completed his secondary education locally, but his parents decided to send him back to India for university when that became due in 1967.

Reflection: Despite the differences in wealth and culture, the people in our house established close, loving, respectful relationships with each other. All the security described could have been set at naught if just one of the half dozen people who worked for us, or anybody they knew, had been persuaded to carry a weapon into the house and use it. None of them had any security protection. They lived either with us or in lines of estate accommodation which benefitted not at all from the dubious cover provided by our SCs. The fact that our staff were all Tamil, very few of whom had joined or sympathised with the largely Chinese MRNLA, may have had something to do with it, as might the relatively good pay and decent treatment they received, but I hope that some of it was genuine affection and loyalty Whatever the motivation, I feel infinitely grateful.

CHAPTER 16

Uplands

Roland is sobbing inconsolably into his father's khaki shorts. In his distress, he notices vaguely that his tears have transferred a large wet stain onto his father's crotch. Very gently, Daddy is detaching Roland's hands from their grip on his legs and transferring them to the gentle but firm grip of Mrs Chaplin, one of Uplands' Indian matrons. Roland is used to being looked after by gentle Indian ladies, and this may be why he allows his father to do this, and then slip quietly away.

Mrs Chaplin shepherds the weeping boy down a flight of steps to the dormitory block and shows him to his bed, made up with crisp white linen, a blanket (for the nights are cool on top of Penang Hill) and pillow. As his sobbing gradually eases, they unpack his trunk together and position his teddy (called Ted) on the bed. Introductions are made to the other 6-year-old boys, and they all trail together through the grounds of the rambling former hotel to the dining hall. There is Nasi Goreng for supper, special food for homesick new boys and girls. Then a sing song and bed- with only a bit of crying under the blanket.

Looking back on my schooldays, I realise how deprived and at the same time how privileged they were. It is clear now that by the early 1950s, and with the occasional blip, such as the assassination of the British High Commissioner in 1951, the British were winning the war (sorry, "Emergency") against the MRNLA. Nevertheless, John and Mary were genuinely concerned about the risk posed to us children by the isolation of

Sungei Toh Pawang Estate.

John was active in the Incorporated Society of Planters, the Planters' trade union, and he was instrumental in establishing Uplands, a boarding school in relatively safe Penang to which British and other expatriate people (and others who could afford it) could entrust their children. It offered (and still does, albeit from premises in Batu Ferringhi, near Georgetown) a British style education at a redundant hotel on Penang Hill, with a temperate climate. It opened in 1955. Boarding schools were at that time a popular way for the middle classes in Britain and its overseas territories to have their children educated; in their view it was obviously out of the question for their children to share the rudimentary schools being established for the local peoples, and anyway, sending your children away to school was absolutely the "done" thing if you could afford it-the tradition of boarding school education for the middle classes remained very strong at this time, for reasons which have always escaped me. I cannot for the life of me see the point of having children if you are going to send them away to spend two thirds of their young lives somewhere else.

When I was 6, in 1957, my parents decided that it was time for me to join the happy band of offspring sent away to school. There was perhaps a grown-up case for reducing the risk to at least one member of the family, and later two when my sister joined me at the age of five, but I found it hard to understand why this was happening when I hadn't, as far as I knew, done anything wrong. Despite the effect of a bout of "Home Leave" I was remarkably close to Devi's family who looked after us and leaving them would be as hard if not harder than leaving my own family. I didn't know then that this would be the last extended time that I would ever live at home in the traditional sense. From this time forward the nature of our family unit changed irrevocably.

The day dawned for my departure. As was usual, all my beloved carers paraded for final farewells. Ramu carefully spat a jet of betel nut juice into the garden before enfolding me in his arms sobbing. And Veloo hung around awkwardly as was his wont. I can remember nothing of my farewell to Devi. After a long journey by road, ferry, and finally funicular railway I found myself up at Uplands with my arms wrapped round my father's khaki shorts wailing my distress at the parting. I must have been disentangled somehow and led away, but I can still remember the damp patch my tears had made on John's long shorts, and years later, when we visited Penang, my stomach still lurched with fear as we passed the bottom station of the Hill Railway.

The school itself was not a cruel place. We were looked after by kindly Indian matrons who slept nearby and comforted our bouts of homesickness without a hint of abuse. There were plenty of places to play, and teaching was good. The joint head teachers were called Mr and Mrs Hawkins, no nonsense expatriate Scots who had taught all over the Empire/Commonwealth. Initially, too, I was collected at weekends to go home, but after a term or two that stopped as well, for reasons which were never made clear, and were the cause of the only tantrum I can ever remember having. Uplands was a decent and humane place, and I'm sure my parents had our best interests at heart, but I don't think I have ever got over the trauma of being separated from them at that age.

To sugar the pill, I was told I could pick a toy to take up to the school at the start of every term, from the colonial department store in Penang called Whiteway Laidlaw. I clearly remember one toy. It was a small plastic sledge, packed with realistic supplies, including petrol cans, water barrels and boxes of all shapes and sizes. The supplies were covered with netting, and behind them stood the sledge driver, holding on to the handles. In front was a team of huskies, 8 I think, all linked to each other and the sledge.

I loved this present; I think the finest thing I ever got. I used to keep it under my pillow in the dormitory at school, and spent hours unpacking and re-packing the supplies, rearranging the dogs, and taking the driver on and off.

As with all childhood presents, it must have got lost at some point but nowadays we would consider what I was doing as play therapy, helping me through the time apart with a link to home.

After a year or so, my sister, aged 5, joined me at Uplands. Now I felt heavily responsible for both of us and can remember bringing her some late-night goodies in her dorm, from a Fourth of July party held for the American kids. I sternly told her that she must not give anything to her friends, but I'm sure she did.

Our new routine was to become the normal pattern of existence; three terms of 10 weeks or so each away from home, with one or two weekends at home and three holiday periods of 4 weeks at Christmas and Easter and 8 weeks in the summer. Necessarily, the distance between my Tamil/Malaysian family and me only got greater. And with my parents too, whose lives continued, largely child free. Not that I was neglected; one or other of them used to write every day, and John's were lavishly illustrated. But their tales of amateur dramatics, church services and curry tiffins were faint echoes of my past life.

There was a point on the path between the dormitories and the dining hall at Uplands where there was a fantastic view down to Georgetown, the island's capital and then across the Straits to the mainland. I would stand here for as long as I could, straining to see if I could catch a glimpse of them, or better still Devi or Ramu. But I never could.

Reflection: The normal "small child at boarding school" narrative always includes abuse of some sort. Mine is not like that; Uplands was a gentle, safe place. No, the pain caused was that of separation from parents, home and everything that represented.

Fig 23: Uplands in the mist

CHAPTER 17

Home Life

Mary Crooke's nursery school is opening for the day. The venue is the ground floor of the Crooke house on Sungei Toh Pawang estate., and it's 8.30. Ramu is bustling round preparing breakfast for John Crooke, newly returned from his morning round of the estate. He breaks down his jungle carbine and takes the clip out of his automatic pistol before settling into his chair at one end of the long black mahogany table. A steady stream of cars is delivering small students to the house front door. But today, hovering at the front door is a young Chinese man with a nervous looking child. Mary stops pouring Ribena blackcurrant juice into cups and welcomes both. The man pushes the child towards Mary and whispers to her. She stands to attention and clearly declaims
"Hickory Dickory Dock
The mouse climbed up the clock.
The clock struck one, the mouse ran down,
Hickory Dickory Dock."
With great presence of mind, Mary applauds enthusiastically, and ushers the child towards a low table with other children round it. No audition piece is required for Mary's school, but the child is pleased, and so is her father.

Fig 24: Mary and her nursery school class

For John and Mary these were years of consolidation in their working lives. In 1960 at the age of 40 John was promoted to Manager of the estate, by which time it must have been clear that the Emergency was winding down. He took over from a fiery Scot called John Cowans, who I was told many years later was involved in multiple fiddles with contractors and suppliers. His main impact on our lives came when he would interrupt my mother's conversations on our shared, party line phone system by shouting "Get off the bloody line, Mary". Oh, and occasionally we would be summoned up to his managerial bungalow on a peak overlooking the estate to take tea with Evelyn, his downtrodden wife.

I like to think that John ran a more honest, calmer ship, a hope encouraged by the affection in which I now know he was held. The cost of the quinquennial home leave described earlier had to be covered, and periodically John found himself doing locum duty on other estates. He would go alone on these gigs, returning at weekends, leaving Mary to look after the home base, with the unfailing support of Devi.

In the mid-1950s, Mary passed a correspondence course in Montessori early years' education. Then she started and ran a nursery school, first in our house, then when it became more popular, at the Sungei Patani Club. Celia and I were attendees before going to the local military school and then Uplands. There were no other schools like this in the area and children from all communities could attend if their parents could afford the modest fees. It became immensely popular as a way of teaching the children English.

A picture, perhaps of a fragmented family, in three different locations.

This period was interrupted twice by the long home leave awarded to European workers every four or five years. My memory is that it was for six months, but two months of that was taken up with the sea voyage either way. In retrospect, each "long leave" marked a further weakening, against my will, of the link between me and what I thought of as my home. I was too young to remember the first one in 1953 or 4 which saw off my ability to speak Tamil, but for the second, in 1958 (a year after I started at Uplands), I remember the family trailing round the country in the back of a Morris Traveller John had hired, moving from relative to relative with varying degrees of welcome.

We would generally be carsick, sometimes to be rescued by John finally locating a National Benzole petrol station. This was apparently the only brand of petrol our Traveller could tolerate, and even then, it was necessary for the attendant- self-service being a thing of the future- to add a squirt of something called Redex, for the spell to work. It was many years before I realised that cars worked equally well on any kind of petrol, apart from the diesel ones, of course.

Given the extent of the Empire at the time, there must have been many families like ours drifting around the country "on leave", so we were not that unusual. Life in the UK seemed somehow more monochrome than at home. I remember not being overly impressed with the grey townscapes and the relative cold, but loving strawberries and cream and Test matches on the radio. Small, cold houses and an absence of servants were minor inconveniences, but I did miss my tropical family. Some families would bring a key servant or two with them on home leave, but this was considered excessively self-indulgent, and said servants always looked cold and confused.

Our 1958 leave included Christmas in that year, and it was a pale shadow of our Christmases in Malaya, which I can still remember- as can Ravi, who talked about them fondly to me 60 years later. There would be a huge tree, decorated by all the children in and around the house. We would wake at silly o'clock to the heavy feeling of a filled stocking lying across our legs. By the time I was 6 I was sceptical about Father Christmas, confirmed by seeing John creep into our room with bunched string stuck to his chin and nose on Christmas night that year. Small presents for the children of the estate supervisory staff, and drinks and mince pies- gingerly tasted and sometimes discarded in favour of the bags of sweets which accompanied them. Carols would be sung, and much of the Christmas booty provided by estate contractors would be redistributed. In later years, as we see, there would be a proper church choir all year round, but the scratch crew my father assembled from other members of the congregation did all right.

Reflection: *The Britain we encountered on home leave never felt like home. It was a strange, grey place, cold and crowded, with none of the vivid warmth of my real home- whether people or landscape. It never occurred to me that sometime soon I would be spending all my time there.*

CHAPTER 18

Blighty Bound

Ramu had prepared two long trestle tables for the 30 or so office and supervisory staff and their wives who had been invited to a farewell curry tiffin for Celia and Roland. The two children, aged 9 and 7 respectively, would be leaving the next day with their mother for the UK, where they would be continuing their education.

Everybody recognised that this would be a defining moment for the children and for the estate community, of which they were a prominent part. In effect they would no longer belong to that community, but were destined to become occasional visitors at best.

This rather undermined John and Mary's efforts to play this event down to their offspring as only a slight change. From now on Roland and Celia would only see their home once a year, for the months of July and August.

Nevertheless, the party went as well as it could. Everybody was in their best clothes, speeches were made, and the children were given expensive cameras (Roland's rather more so than Celia's).

But what the children were really dreading was tomorrow's goodbyes to those closest to them- Devi and Ramu. They had done this before, going to Uplands, but this would be much, much worse.

Fig 23: (l to r) Ramu, Roland (12), Devi and Celia (10) just before
the dreaded return to school.

Then, when I was 9, there came the final severance from my real home, and the journey back "home" to school in England. There was only so far an English model school in the tropics was considered capable of taking an expatriate child's education in the late 50s.

In 1960 I would be 10, only 3 years away from the age at which I would be entered for the Common Entrance exam which admitted you to public (i.e., private secondary) school. High time therefore that I joined the proper British private educational system, as opposed to the pale tropical imitation offered by Uplands. John and Mary, as products of their time and class, would not have considered remotely adequate the more local alternatives; closest would have been the British Forces' secondary school in Singapore(in effect a state secondary modern) or a whole range of schools in Australia.

School in Singapore, or even perhaps in Oz, would have allowed me to go home every holiday, but this counted for nothing when set against the gold standard of education in the U.K., as viewed by the British expatriate middle classes

The expense of air travel, and the penny-pinching of John's employers, meant that Celia and I would spend only the long summer holiday at home. The rest of the year would be spent either at school, or with "guardians" yet to be arranged- of which more later. The local estate community understood well that this would be a major and final departure and a grand farewell tea party was arranged.

This is Mary's account of the party. As I remember it, I wasn't quite as directive towards my sister as Mary makes me out to be. There were upwards of 30 staff and their spouses, sitting at long tables in front of the house. But she captures the shared sadness of the occasion, and reading her account now, I do sense her regret at what was going to happen., and awareness of the significance of the occasion.

We remember.

Roland, dressed in shirt and tie and long trousers eyed his sister in a dainty Thai silk dress.

"You'd better sit at the bottom of the table- would you like to speak too?"

"Well, of course, I'll say thank you too".

"Well, don't take too long, and wait till I've finished"

This was the briefing before the farewell party to both our children before we three flew "home" where they would start at their English boarding schools. The office and estate staff had asked to come up and present a gift to them and tell them how much they would be missed in the life of our plantation.

"We are wanting to wish them luck and happiness despite the unhappiness of leaving their home... We know they will be back..."

Ramu calmly produced a curry fit for a king and thus acceptable to the men and their wives, most of whom would have experienced the same pain of separation when their children went off to India, and sometimes even Australia for higher education.

Mr Lim, the chief clerk, rose at the end of the meal, and spoke of their love and admiration for Roland and Celia, how they had grown up on the estate, and been part of its life. He prayed for their future happiness and then sat down. No presents? Then everyone looked at John who said

"Roland would like to speak to you"

Roland rose shyly but confidently- at this stage I was seized by doubts- hadn't he planned to say something on the lines of "thank you for the lovely presents you have given, we shall treasure them etc etc"

But with the aplomb and timing of a more mature person he launched forth:

"Thank you all for coming. Celia and I will always remember you and the friendship you have given us will be forever. Now Celia would like to say something."

"Oh, thank you for coming. It is so kind and we will always remember you"!

They all then rose and from the cars were brought two parcels which were presented to R and C as everyone said goodbye. R said to his father "Shall I use the other speech now?!"

The presents were a then state of the art Zeiss Ikon box camera, which I used for some years, and a slightly less exotic Kodak Brownie camera for Celia. This had a short strap which Celia always used to keep wound round her wrist. The cost of these two pieces of advanced tech would have been considerable, even shared among the office staff, and I have always appreciated the sacrifice made to buy them for us.

More painful than the office staff tea party were the farewells to Devi and her family, to Ramu, Maniam and the others. From now on we would see them once a year, for 8 weeks, and our ways would part for good.

Reflection: My overwhelming feeling about this event at this distance is how it should never have happened. I believe the chain of assumptions which resulted in people who could ill afford the expenditure ending up paying for expensive cameras for their boss's children goes like this:

1. *These children require primary and secondary education.*
2. *The only possible way in which they can receive that education is at boarding schools in the UK*
3. *Therefore, they must leave their home and travel to the UK where they will stay.*
4. *Therefore, we must mark this event with a present.*
5. *Since Orang Puteh already have most things, it had better be a pretty expensive one.*

CHAPTER 19

Guardians

Aunt Pat's little car turns carefully into the playground of Clapham Park School for partially sighted children. It is the first week of the Autumn term, and Celia and Roland can still just about recall their last swim in the Harvard Club pool and saying goodbye to Devi and Veloo. Next week they will be back at their boarding schools, but the prospect ahead of them now is of reading in a disused classroom until break or lunch. The only excitement will happen if the boy living with epilepsy has one of his fits, which are excitingly active episodes of falling, shaking and shouting which the boy doesn't ever recall. His classmates are utterly phlegmatic, and well used to placing him in the recovery position and Roland and Celia learn it too.

This is better than spending the day with Pat's elderly friends, who are both very deaf, and whose house always smells of cabbage. Soon their terms will start, their tuck boxes will be loaded onto their respective trains and they will be once again counting off the very many days until they return home (without inverted commas).

Our journey "home" and insertion into English boarding school life was supervised by Mary, and I remember little of our final departure and the flight.

We landed at Heathrow in early January, and Celia and I were utterly unprepared for how grey and dingy England appeared to be, or how cold it was. Jetlagged, we didn't really sleep, and both got into Mary's bed in the early hours to listen to the alien noises of traffic and the milkman making his deliveries.

John and Mary had chosen separate boarding schools for each of us, the concept of co-education being in its infancy. Celia's, called Manor House, was near Wimborne in Dorset. Mine, Durlston was in a tiny seaside village in Hampshire. The plan was for Mary to stay in the UK until the summer, when John would join her for the holidays, before both returned to Malaysia in the Autumn. We would be at our respective schools for the Autumn, Spring and Summer terms to get us used to the experience and to get to know our guardians, who would be in loco parentis from the Autumn of 1961.

With all of us expat children at boarding school, there was the issue of who was to be in loco parentis in the UK, to act as a point of contact for the schools in the days before the Internet and put us up for any holidays during which we were not joining our parents (Christmas and Easter in our case). Usually, the job was done by relatives; grandparents or uncles/aunts, but in our family we didn't have any suitable candidates- which is ironic considering who we did get. On both John's and Mary's side there were no grandfathers, and all uncles were either a) living abroad and/or b) fully childrened already.

Our guardians, or "the Aunts", as we were encouraged to call them, were Pat Horne, my godmother, unmarried head teacher at a school for the partially sighted, in her 30s, and the older Mary Horton, a widowed supervisor at a posh clothing maker. Pat was the sister of Derek Horne, the Captain in the Black Watch regiment who had been engaged to marry Mary but who had been killed in Normandy at the Falaise Gap battle in the summer of 1944.

I don't know when or how Pat and Mary met, but by the time we were entrusted to their care they had set up home together, and in retrospect it is obvious that they were a couple. In those days, this sort of arrangement, though not unlawful thanks to Queen Victoria refusing to accept that lesbianism was possible, was highly unusual, and it would certainly have been outside the experience of John and Mary. Celia and I must have been greatly incurious because I don't remember wondering about the relationship at all. There were certainly undercurrents of tension in their relationship which impacted mostly on Celia, and these became worse over the next few years. In the end our care was switched to an equally unsuitable but much more entertaining person- of whom more later.

Pat and Mary lived in a little terraced house in Carshalton, Surrey. Pat was definitely our primary carer, and her own career as head teacher at a school for partially sighted children meant that at the beginning and end of the two holidays we were with her in the year, Christmas and Easter, there was always a bit of an issue about what we were going to do during the extra bits of those holidays which as private school kids we had over and above that enjoyed by her students. Sometimes we would spend them with elderly friends of the Aunts, sometimes we would be deposited in unused classrooms to while away the day. Either way, it was not a lot of fun, and we looked forward longingly to our summer holiday.

Fig 24: Tea with the 'Aunts' and longing for the holidays...

Celia and I were both at reasonably humane boarding schools in the south of England, and the vagaries of international air travel at the time meant that we were released a few days early at the end of the summer term to catch our flight. We travelled together usually, but I remember some annoying delays to leaving due to having to stay overnight with the aunts before and after the holiday, at the insistence of our parents for diplomatic reasons; "They're very fond of you, darling, and it's not much to ask, really".

Yes, it was. We hadn't seen our home or our parents for many months and couldn't see why the feelings of people who were being paid to look after us were so important.

Reflection: It's hard to convey how important our annual 8 weeks in Malaya/Malaysia were to us. For 44 weeks a year we lived lives away from our true homes and families, but those 8 summer weeks were a chance to re-immerse and reattach ourselves to those things. With hindsight, I can see that for the Aunts we were precious family substitutes, that they desperately wanted us to view them also as parents, and that they must have been terribly hurt whenever it seemed that we weren't doing so. But they weren't our parents, and we would never see them as such. The same applied to Holly, our other guardian, though she brought a whole different package of world view and emotional baggage to the party.

CHAPTER 20

Prep School

The bell goes for the end of the lesson before break. The boys tumble out of the classroom, and dash to a patch of scrubland on the other side of the playground. Through some arcane process involving showing each other clenched fists and fingers one of them marches to the mud heap in the middle of the patch. The rest scatter to various points in and around the school buildings and playground and start creeping towards the mud heap. All are wearing an identical uniform of blue dungarees fastened by one strap, and a navy sweatshirt. They try to hide their faces from the boy on the heap; if he identifies them, they must return to their starting point. If they can get across an imaginary line drawn around the mud heap, they only have to touch him without being first touched and they have won the right to occupy the mud heap for the next round. It is a brilliant game, and Roland is enormously proud of having invented it.

My school was a small preparatory school on the south coast. It was surrounded by trees which grew at a 45-degree angle in deference to the prevailing gale force winds. There was a sprinkling of colonial kids like me, and a few staff ("masters" to us) who carried titles like Captain, Major, or in one exalted case, Colonel. It was only 15 years since the end of hostilities in World War 2, but as well as slightly shell-shocked vets we also had masters who had been through National Service.

My arrival caused a bit of a stir because of my dark skin. Word got about that I was a refugee who had been supplied to the school by Oxfam; this didn't result in the expected bullying, largely because despite my dusky appearance, my English was perfect, and I clearly had no difficulties with the syllabus. I avoided the inevitable reoriented persecution as a swot and brainbox, as I did throughout my school career, by ensuring that I made the occasional mistake, helping the really thick boys with their prep and telling only slightly fanciful tales about my life in Malaya.

There was a lot of reading aloud in rotation. As some of my comrades stumbled slowly through Rider Haggard, I had normally finished the book and was reading another one until it was my turn. I took to French and Latin like a duck to water; my only weak points lay in Science, which I always felt I was on the brink of understanding, but never quite did.

Every Friday evening there was a film show, with the projector operated by one of the shell-shocked masters. It generally broke down two or three times to loud groans from us boys and sometimes the show would be abandoned as the master was led away sobbing.

On Saturday mornings there would be an assembly at which each master would read a report on his (or her, we had one female teacher, who wasn't called a mistress, much to my disappointment) form or activity. If the dread words "Blenkinsop major (the oldest brother at the school was "major", the second "minor", and the third "minimus") is LAZY" were uttered, said Blenkinsop would have to stand up and remain standing until the end of the assembly.

I managed to avoid this fate; indeed, I still possess 7 embossed books which were awarded every term to a few of us for hard work. As I write this, I marvel that all this swotty, creepy activity never branded me as a bullying victim.

We now know that places like my school in the 60s, 70s and even 80s were hotbeds of paedophilia, but I seemed to largely avoid that too, despite my fetching dark skin and curly hair. Stereotypically, the music master and the chaplain (yes, we had one of those) I now recognise as being pederasts. The chaplain used to have us boys into his room to sit on his rather large bed while he read a story, but I remember no untoward activity- maybe it happened when I wasn't there.

The music master did once sit me on his knee to ask me to join or stay in the choir- I said no, but don't remember being particularly upset by the gesture. Other than that, I recall nothing untoward, but then the climate of the times was, I am ashamed to say now, broadly tolerant of child abuse. Both my prep school and my public (i.e. private)school permitted staff and senior boys to beat children with a range of implements, from slippers, through knotted towels to bamboo canes as punishment. Again, I managed to escape this tradition right up until the last couple of years of my public-school career- about which more later.

Prep school involved quite a bit of unsupervised free time during which we roamed the grounds of the school playing variants of games involving shooting each other with pretend weapons. There was always a lot of argument about who had shot who first and how long you had to be dead before rejoining the battle. We never left the school grounds, but occasionally the outside intruded. On one occasion a rumour swept the school that teddy boys, the early 60s version of hooligans, had invaded. Despite, or perhaps because of, stern instructions to stay away, we flocked there, whereupon one of the ex-army officers ordered us to lie prone, for reasons which escape me, but may have been his military training kicking in.

On another, there was rumoured to be a smoking gang at large in the cricket pavilion and some of us made it our mission to round them up and turn them in. I do not think we ever managed to catch these hardened criminals.

But my major achievement at Durlston was the invention of a cool game. Called, rather unimaginatively, "Touch the Mudheap", it involved stalking, pursuit and concealment in an area of the school grounds next to the main official playground. One of us (usually me, it was my game after all) stood on the eponymous mudheap. The other players had to start at the outer edge of an outer ring round the mudheap. Once they entered this ring, whether walking, crawling (advisable) or running, they could be sent back to the start line if spotted and identified by the mudheap occupant. This was more difficult than it seems because we all wore identical blue dungarees for play and if you curled up on the ground it was difficult to differentiate one boy from another.

Once you had made it into the inner zone around the mudheap, identification no longer mattered. Now your task was to reach the mudheap untagged by its occupant. Again, more feasible than it seems when you consider that 2 or 3 boys might be making their end runs at the same time. Brilliant game.

Every weekend we had to write a letter to our parents. Mary and John were faithful in each writing to me every week, as they had at Uplands; my father's efforts were usually illustrated by him. There exists an example of my letter to them from prep school, which includes the fascinating information that we had watched professional wrestling (this and Dr Who were, for some reason, the only programmes we were allowed to watch, but I found them entrancing, never having watched TV before).

Fig 25: My letter home

Durlston Court,
Barton-on-Sea,
Hants,
22-1-61.

Dear Mummy,
    I hope you are well. It's not bad at Durlston, but I am still a bit home-sick. We saw a film last night called "Angels one five". It was about a pilot who kept on doing wrong things and at last died in combat. We also saw a comedy. I played football yesterday and I was right back. I am in Marlborough Dormitory. I enclose a letter to Daddy and maybe one to Celia. Thank you for your letter and thank Miggy for her post card. We go to chapel each evening. Give my love to Miggy.
                    Love From
                        Roland.

P.T.O.

Reflection: *Like Uplands, my prep school was a gentle, slightly eccentric place. This was largely due to its headmaster, who, if he heard of a distinction awarded to an alumnus of his school, would award a half day's holiday. These distinctions didn't have to be terribly major, with the result that by the end of term there could be three or four half day holidays still to be taken. The deputy head, who was made of sterner stuff, would then consolidate all outstanding holidays into one, much to the chagrin of the boys. There were several boys like me with families abroad, and we were, I think, rather envied for our exotic backgrounds, and ability to leave school early in* *the summer to catch planes. For our part, we felt less angst at the start of the spring and summer terms than other boys because we were not being wrenched away from hearth and home and had this other dimension to our lives. It remains the case however that in my view, boarding schools are a form of child abuse which parents should be ashamed of inflicting on their children.*

CHAPTER 21

Endless Summer

The Church of St Philip and St James is unusual for its time and place. The Anglican Church in Sungei Patani, Malaysia in the mid-60s still largely caters for the expatriate community. Its local congregations are largely Indian and Chinese. St Philip and St James has an Australian priest and an English choir master. John Crooke has always loved singing and has assembled an enthusiastic band of young local people to form a multiracial choir. Several of the choir members are from the Ebenezer family, Christians from South India, who relish the excitement of weekly rehearsals and then Sunday services, which often include dramatic re-imaginings of biblical and social situations.

When Roland and Celia come out for the summer they are co-opted into the choir and join the summer social highlight of the choir's season- the Barbecue, where there is much cheeky teasing of the choir master, while sausages and burgers cook over a split oil drum with a metal grille stretched over it.

Fig 26: St Philip and St James Church Choir, c1966

It is hard to exaggerate how unusual this scene would have been at the time, as Malaysia was transitioning from a colonial past to a post-colonial future. As Mangla (nee Ebenezer) says in her contribution, the friendships made then and there "have endured until the present day."

For most of the interminable summer term all I could think about was going home. Our first solo trip was to Singapore, courtesy of the British Overseas Airways Corporation, on the then bang up to date Douglas DC 7C, a 4-engine propeller driven aircraft which took 23 hours (compared with 12 now) and made stops in Beirut and Bombay before reaching its destination. Most of the passengers were children like us, flying out to join parents in South East Asia. We all had badges saying "Unaccompanied Minor", which in retrospect must have been a bit like wearing bullseye targets for predatory adults. They mostly got ditched as we celebrated our release from boarding school. Things became quite rowdy, and the cabin crew were reduced to locking us all in transit lounges at our airport stops.

Celia to this day suffers badly from travel sickness. On this inaugural flight she was sick 9 times, handing the last offering to a steward as she got off the plane. We were greeted by John, who had travelled down to Singapore alone because Mary didn't trust her ability to remain composed in public. I remember John greeting us in calm, but clearly pleased to see us way. He didn't give way to emotion much, but he must have been in internal turmoil.. Then we boarded the Night Mail train, which plied between Singapore and, eventually, Bangkok. I can remember that journey very clearly, the unique sounds and scent of Malaya at night, equal parts rotting vegetation and damp soil with the sounds of cicadas and other nameless creatures. The rhythm of the train would put you to sleep, only to wake when it pulled into stations, and the sheer gut-wrenching excitement of knowing that early the next day you would be *home*.

The Night Mail got into Bukit Mertajam station, southeast of Penang, a little after 5am. We got off, in a Brief Encounter style cloud of steam, to find Mary, with Veloo hanging about awkwardly just off centre, clutching a pair of sunglasses she had worn to ward off a display of emotion. Veloo picked up one of the lighter bags and strode off towards the car while slightly restrained hugs were exchanged.

No restraint an hour later when we found Devi and Ramu, and Maniam and Sinayah, the two gardeners, standing waiting to greet us outside the house. I can still remember the overwhelming flood of emotion on greeting them both, all of us in tears and leaking streams of snot- betel nut tinged in Ramu's case.

From then on, the holiday cleaved to a well-worn path. Most days were spent at Harvard swimming club on the neighbouring estate. Sunday evenings were spent in church in Sungei Patani, followed by supper at Ma Brown's restaurant. Sometimes there would be a curry tiffin party on another estate, though these became less frequent as expat planters began to leave in the mid-60s.

The local Anglican church of St Philip and St James in Sungei Patani was central to John and Mary's life. John raised a choir, initially from the expatriate community and then from local Anglicans. The core of this choir by the mid-60s was a local family called Ebenezer, whose four daughters and two sons were all members. Here is an appreciation of John sent to me by one of those choristers:

Memories from the heart, by Mangla Ebenezer

My early memories of John Crooke, whom we fondly called Mr Crooke was in the early 60s. I was in my early teens. He came by our house to seek my parents' approval to recruit my siblings and I to join the Choir which he was going to start in our local church, St Philip and St James. The church was in an isolated kampong in Sungei Petani, called Sungei Layar. He straightaway got my parents approval for us to join the choir. My parents knew all of us had good voices to give to God and it will also keep us away from mischief.

Mr Crooke started having choir practices every Friday which started around 5pm and ended before 6pm. He managed to recruit at least 15 youths to sing in the choir. He and his wife Mary always made sure we reached home safely. Most of the time he would send us home in his "Holden". What a joy when he used to call us "The Ebenezers" to get into his car. We were always taken on jolly rides to Penang and had ice cream at a snack bar.

Mr Crooke was kind, gentle and a man of compassion. Though he was a planter at Sungei Toh Pawang Estate he showed such humility. During choir practices he was a no-nonsense man. We had to be punctual, listen carefully to his voice training as he trained us to sing in parts. He used to commend me by saying that I sang like a nightingale. I was chosen to sing Soprano and the best part is I still sing in the choir.

He was also the stalwart of the church and held high offices within the local government. He was awarded the Justice of Peace and had good relationship with the late Sultan of Kedah. During summer holidays in UK his children Roland and Celia would come down to Malaysia to spend time with their parents. John and Mary would organise a Barbeque night and most of the choir members would attend and have fun and meet their children who were about my age. We developed a bond of friendship and have maintained it till today.

John and Mary left for UK after his retirement in the late 60s. It was a tearful farewell as we bade them goodbye. We kept in touch through letters which brought much joy as we were still connected. In the 70s I went to pursue my nursing course in UK and I was blessed to visit them in their home in Somerset and spent a few days with them.

We were sad to hear of John's passing away in 1987. But our family continued to keep in touch with Mary and even visited her when on holiday in late 90s. John Crooke served God well in his home, community and church. I shall conclude with this Biblical verse. Mathew 25 verse 21 says: His Lord said to him, "Well done thou good and faithful servant, you were faithful over a few things, I will make you a ruler of many things. Enter into the joy of your Lord".

Sometimes there would be trips to Penang. I would ignore the sinking feeling going past the funicular railway station and memories of travelling on it to school at Uplands and enjoy instead swimming in the saltwater pools at the Penang Swimming Club.

Every Monday, Mary would put in her order to Barkath's the grocers in Butterworth. These always started the same way: "Two pounds soup bones, two pounds soup meat. One pound ox heart, one pound ox tripe". These were the ingredients for the dogs' dinners, but we thought it hilariously funny to chorus them as she spoke. I don't suppose Barkath's did.

Our eight weeks holiday were a precious respite from our alien existence in the UK. Of course, we could not recover the closeness and intimacy of our friendships from before; Santha and Vasantha by this time were married and living elsewhere locally, and the eldest brother Pany was a Medical worker on another estate. But Ravi, Devi, Veloo and Ramu remained as fixed points and reminders of our previous life. We continued the tradition of meals taken with Devi and any of her visiting children. Breakfasts of puthu, a mixture of coconut and rice flour steamed and topped with coconut sugar or appam, a lacy pancake eaten with curry. Best of all, this nectar was to be eaten with our hands- right hands only, though according to custom.

Ramu would retaliate with his repertoire of western and local dishes, including the best roast potatoes I have ever eaten. He was entirely self-taught. Our family meals were taken at a huge shiny rectangular black table, John and I sitting at top and bottom and Mary and Celia on the other two sides. John would carve or serve the main course, and Ramu would circulate dressed in white shirt, full length sarong and bare feet, holding a tureen in each hand: serving Mary first, then Celia, then John, then me. He always lingered by Celia and me, silently urging us with his chin (it's considered rude in Indian culture to point using your finger) to take another morsel. We used to compete to make him giggle and threaten the stability of his tureens, but he never dropped one.

He worked from early morning, making morning tea and breakfast until after lunch, when he used to cycle off to his quarters on Division 1 of the estate for a rest and a bath, returning in the early evening to serve drinks and dinner. I don't remember him ever having a full day off when we were there, but on Sundays he took the afternoon off, and didn't work when we were away.

There were also fixed events; a week at Batu Ferringhi beach in Penang, at one of the only two hotels there at the time (now there are many huge tower resorts) Golden Sands or Lone Pine, and one week at the Cameron Highlands, a hill resort in the next door state of Perak. Batu Ferringhi was a week of swimming and sunbathing, while Cameron Highlands, with its temperate climate, was jungle walks, visits to a pig farm, golf (the only place John and Mary would play) and log fires in the evenings.

Going to the Camerons involved getting up early and setting off with sandwiches Ramu had made for us. These were always wrapped, at Mary's insistence, in slightly damp muslin, giving a rather unpleasant clammy texture to lunch, which was always eaten as we crossed the Perak river inter state boundary. Shortly thereafter we would start the ascent to the Camerons, with the inevitably consequent vomiting from the back seat.

Eventually we would arrive at the Kedah State Rest House. As in other British colonies, there was in Malaya a network of bungalows and houses for European government servants to use, primarily for duty purposes, but also for vacations and relaxation (thus "Rest"). They were always staffed and could be booked, as we did, for holiday purposes. The additional restriction which applied to the Camerons' rest house was that it was the Kedah Sultan's official holiday residence, and one bedroom, particularly large and lavishly furnished, was not to be used. But Cookie (see below) used to let us into to eyeball the sumptuous appointments, allowing us to pretend to be the Sultan and Sultanah.

When we arrived at Kedah House after what seemed like hours of winding hairpin bends and serial vomiting, we would be welcomed by its Chinese cook, nicknamed, imaginatively, Cookie.

Lunch was always the same: Steak and eggs, followed by the little alpine strawberries that grew at that altitude. There would be a roaring fire in the grate, and we would all be wearing cardigans or jumpers in the evening. By this point, this was not so much of a treat for Celia and me, accustomed as we were to the chillier UK climes, as it was for John and Mary, but it was still cosy and a relief from the utterly regular daily humid heat of the lowlands.

Inevitably, the endless summer holiday would eventually come to an end, and we would reverse the arrival itinerary in something of a depression. We bitterly resented having to return a day or two early to allow the Aunts some face time, but as was usually the case, Celia was somewhat more vocal than me about it.

Reflection: John Crooke's choir was an unusual, joyful thing. John seemed to have an affinity for the enthusiastic young people in it. For them it would have been unusual to have a relationship with an expat like him, happy to teach them and encourage them, making choral singing fun, but also arranging barbecues and trips to the city.

Mangla speaks of his "humility", a word often attached to him.

CHAPTER 22

All Change

Roland and the other three new bugs are sitting at the long tables used for prep (homework) in the B House Junior Common Room. They are waiting for the clock's hands to get to 4.30pm, the appointed hour for high tea with Murf, the bachelor housemaster.

Murf's house is accessed by an almost vertical path up the hillside from B House. Once there, they shuffle around outside the front door until Murf yells "Come" in a stentorian voice. They find themselves in the open kitchen of a modern timber frame house. Preparations have already begun- a dozen eggs broken into a bowl with a huge knob of butter in there as well; rashers of bacon and chipolata sausages, and crumpets on toasting forks ready for incineration in front of a fire.

The boys each find themselves in charge of one of the elements of their tea, with Murf moving them round at random. Eventually everything is on big plates in the dining room and they are being ordered to help themselves before toasting crumpets and consuming those as well.

Dishes are cleared away and the beetle-browed house master brings out a small box with 2 packs of cards. This is the game of Pit, based loosely on open outcry in a commodities exchange. It requires players to collect one of a few commodities, such as wheat or corn, by process of shouting what they have available to swap.

Murf makes this process more exciting by cheating outrageously. Initially, when the boys notice this, they say nothing, out of a combination of fear and respect. Eventually, Roland nervously ventures something like "excuse me sir, that wasn't quite right.......", to

*be greeted with outraged affront by the housemaster, followed swiftly
by an ostentatious wink to the other boys.*

*When eventually they are packed off back to B House they are
well fed and more relaxed than they have so far been in the intimidating week they have been at Bradfield.*

In 1964, I was 13, and in the fashion decreed for generations of middle-class boys, I moved from Durlston to Bradfield
College, having passed common entrance- not well enough to
get a scholarship, which John and Mary were hoping for to reduce the cost of my education (I was awarded a scholarship, for
one third of the fees, in the next year). My renewed pleas to attend a school in Singapore or Australia were gently ignored by
my parents.

I was, though, given some say as to which public school
I went to. As I recall, it came down to a choice between Sherborne School in Dorset and Bradfield College (it was immensely
proud of being a college) in Berkshire. I went for Bradfield, because their winter team sports were soccer and hockey, while
Sherborne's were rugby and rugby. I hated rugby and had got
through games at Durlston by running fluently into positions
where nobody could throw the ball to me, then expressing loud
disappointment that I had been missed out. The rule was that
you had to get your knees dirty in games, so towards the end, if
I had escaped involvement, I would sink discreetly to my knees
to achieve the desired effect.

Bradfield was founded originally in the mid-19th century
to provide officer class recruits to the Church of England priest-
hood. This had been somewhat diluted by the early 60s, but the
weekly routine included attendance at Chapel in the morning,
daily, as well as house prayers in the evening, a communion service for those who had been confirmed on Wednesday morning,
and a church service on Sunday.

The school did not have a uniform, but new boys (new
bugs) were required to wear dark grey flannel trousers of a
particular type (Van Heusen, I think) and a restricted range of

sports jackets (and woe betide you if you wore the wrong sort). Underneath the jacket we had to wear collarless shirts with separate collars, which attached to the back of the shirt with a collar stud. You could imagine the potential for disaster if you lost a stud or ran out of collars. Shirts would become extremely grimy and smelly and there was a flourishing black market in studs. With the shirt was worn a house tie or on Sundays a college tie (or the other way around, I can't remember- either way getting it wrong was painful). Unless you were a scholar you could not undo your jacket buttons. Once you got into the sixth form you could dispense with the ghastly collarless shirts, and switch to ones like normal people wore. Apparently. Everybody had to wear black academic gowns on top of the jacket and trouser combo, and the competition here was to make your gown as tatty and soiled as possible by using it to mop up ink, food, drink - anything, really.

The College's (never school) non-uniform code made me and the other new bugs in B House (imaginatively, the various accommodation houses were listed from A to H) look a little like a flock of very small university lecturers. The English public school house system was based on a vague theory that they could recreate a family atmosphere, by grouping 30 or so boys in a building where they would sleep, socialise, and do their prep (homework), under the care of a housemaster.

Ours was called Murray Argyle, nicknamed Murf. He was a gruff, rotund man of medium height, who I first met properly when the other new bugs and I were summoned to tea on the first Sunday afternoon. I had had a difficult first week; John had once again done the honours and delivered me to school. I don't think I disgraced myself on this occasion; I had after all been delivered to Durlston by Mary, which made a change in the pattern of parental abandonment, and this parting had been made slightly more agonising by the fact that at 13 I wasn't supposed to blub (cry). This, despite seeing him disappear for tea into the house of one of the masters who we knew socially when I thought he had gone.

The Sunday tea ritual was Murf's amazingly effective way of inducting homesick new boys. We climbed the hill above B House to his bachelor quarters in a modern bungalow. There we were instructed as a group to cook the sausages, bacon, and scrambled egg, and make the toast and tea, while Murf prowled around giving more or less helpful hints about speeding up or improving the quality of the product. It was difficult to mope when this sort of activity was happening, and after tea, Murf would lead a riotous game of Pit, a popular card game at the time based on shouting bids for various primary products. He would cheat outrageously; we would glance at each other and finally the bravest would very tentatively (Sir, sir, sir) challenge him. He would pretend to be outraged, while winking ostentatiously. Worked every time.

Another part of our induction was a requirement to learn about all aspects of the College, including its traditions stretching back not that long to 1856, nicknames of the staff and key locations in the various buildings. For some reason, it was also necessary to know the routes of all the cross country runs, such as "Buscot-River", being a route round through the village of Buscot, returning along the river Pang, and the much sought after "River-River", being out and back along the Pang, and our shortest run. To aid this learning, we were each allocated a "nurse", who would test us on the dossier we had to learn.

After four weeks we were tested by four "beaks", house prefects-(one step down from "cops" who wielded supreme power as school prefects, wore white ties as a badge of office and sat in a special side pew in chapel. They would enter last, just before the masters, and leave first, just after the masters, in a whirl of slightly soiled black gowns). Passing this test was essential for your own standing in the house, and that of your nurse, and thankfully, I did.

Reflection: Bradfield was the third boarding school I had been to and my arrival there marked the seventh year of being educated away from home. The separation now from John and Mary was year-

long and also inter-continental and marked the further loosening of my ties with home. I missed them and my local family immensely, and navigating adolescence was much harder without that support. But it wasn't unusual at that time, and one was expected to get on with it without making too much of a fuss. I was becoming used by now to a life largely independent from my parents, though it was to take its toll later.

CHAPTER 23

Beginning of the End

Gerti Hollitscher is taking her usual daily constitutional walk along the seafront at Douglas, on the Isle of Man. This section has been fenced off and barbed wire barriers placed at either end, and within it are held the British residents of German and Austrian origin and refugees from those countries who have been interned while their background and bona fides are checked. She is 40 years old and has been in Britain for two years. She hasn't heard from her family in Vienna for nearly a year; discreet enquiries with non-Jewish neighbours indicate that they have been rounded up for deportation and their apartment allocated to a Nazi official.

Her fellow internees are the cream of pre-war Jewish society in Germany and Austria, as well as non-Jews who have been living in Britain for years. Soon, the British authorities will come to their senses and she will be released, along with the members of the Amadeus string quartet who met on the Island. Gerti is desperate both to practice medicine and fight back against the Nazis who have abducted and probably killed her family. On release she will effectively picket the office of the officer responsible for recruitment to the Royal Army Medical Corps, until he agrees to let her enlist. She will serve throughout the war in various theatres, and then in the Colonial medical service in Malaya, where she meets John and Mary.

By this time proudly British, she will remain eccentrically and exotically foreign, refusing to let language, or increasing blindness stand in her way. Roland loves her very much.

By 1964, John's and Mary's lives in Malaysia, as it now

was, were well established, despite the gradual departure of other expats and the reduction in the size of the estate as Eastern Industries, the owners, sold bits off. In that year, the family moved from the house that John had seen from his cattle wagon on the way north to the Siam Burma Railway, on Division 1 of the estate, which was sold lock, stock and barrel, to a new one on Division 2. John had started a choir in the church of St Philip and St James, a new branch of Rotary International, and had been made a Justice of the Peace by the Sultan of Kedah. Mary ran a remarkably successful nursery school, and they were both prominent members of the church community. They continued to write to Celia and me weekly, each of them, and we were also required by the school to write weekly in return.

In a brief, back to the future-style interlude, Indonesia refused to recognise the establishment of the Federation of Malaysia in 1962 and threatened to invade. This period, known as Konfrontasi or Confrontation in Indonesian, involved incursions into East Malaysia and several unsuccessful parachute landings in peninsula Malaysia , all of which were seen off by combined Commonwealth and Malaysian forces. Sungei Toh Pawang Estate staff patrolled the estate at night to report any nocturnal arrivals by Indonesian forces.

Interracial tensions surfaced on the estate in 1966, when the estate shop, leased and managed by an ex-rubber tapper, was robbed by two Malays from a local village. They were armed; despite theoretically high penalties for illegally held arms, there were still many weapons in circulation which had been held by SCs and other security force personnel demobilized once the Emergency had ended. The shopkeeper was shot and killed in the attack, as was an estate lorry driver who rushed into the shop to help. John was convinced that the police, also mostly Malay, had made little effort to catch the perpetrators despite his lobbying the senior local police commander. He campaigned hard for the shopkeeper's widow to be given compensation from a state fund set up for this purpose, and for the courage of the shopkeeper's two assistants also to be recognised. As local Justice of the Peace, he presided at a ceremony when these awards were made and publicised in the press, in the presence of the shamefaced local police commander.

But the high tide of empire had been reached years earlier, and the increasingly assertive Malay dominated government of the new Federation of Malaysia was determined to Malaysianise the economy. Malay was made the national language, and British civil servants and managers were replaced in a largely friendly, peaceful process. In John's case, large parts of the estate were sold, and we moved houses to the part remaining under his management. Most other European managers were being replaced by Malaysian citizens.

As far as Celia and I were concerned, our guardianship by the aunts was becoming untenable. The focus of unhappiness was Celia's relationship with Mary Horton. Both women were very keen to be regarded as proper parents to us, for reasons which are not hard to divine, and in a variety of ways we resisted their imperative. In the four-sided relationship, I regarded myself as responsible for Celia, and while I got on well with Pat and was able to tolerate Mary, Celia found Mary's aspirations to parenthood particularly difficult and there were frequent rows. Things were not always tense; when supper time came around, we would sometimes be presented with a handwritten menu of choices. These would be a variety of things on toast which could be easily rustled up, but we loved, after weeks of following orders at school, being able to decide what we wanted. And we would get half a crown pocket money every Saturday which we could spend at the sweetshop in the same street.

But we knew who our parents were, and it wasn't them. I think that, by early 1964, even my rather unworldly parents had also begun to think that there was something a bit unusual for the time about Pat and Mary's set up; for instance, the fact that they shared a room, and John and Mary certainly knew about the tensions between us and them.

Why John and Mary thought the answer to the guardianship problem was Holly, I do not know. If you had to draw up a list of desirable qualities in a guardian to two teenage children, Holly would have had practically none of them.

Dr Gertrud Hollitscher MD (Vienna) was a redoubtable single, middle-aged lady of Austrian extraction, now proudly British, as she would remind anybody who made the mistake of asking about her origins. Part of a large liberal Jewish family, she qualified as a doctor in the 1930s, and judging by her medical interventions with us, seemed not to have learnt anything since. Her father had, like many in his community, seen the writing on the wall, and dispatched her to London shortly before the Anschluss (the absorption of Austria into the Greater German Reich). Her entire family, save a second cousin, perished in the Holocaust. Holly was left as the sole representative of her family, in an alien country.

Like all German-speaking refugees, Holly (as she was known to her English-speaking friends, Gerti to her central European ones) was interned, in a huge piece of unfair idiocy, by the British authorities in the Isle of Man on the outbreak of war. When the penny finally dropped, after several months, that most German speaking people in the UK at that time were not 5th columnists for the Nazis, they were released. Thus, for example the Amadeus string quartet, who met on the island, were formed, and played throughout the war. Holly's contribution was to join the Royal Army Medical Corps and serve as a doctor on various fronts. It was to say the least highly unusual for a female, foreign doctor to be allowed to serve, and Holly used to claim that she only managed it because she sat outside the door of the officer responsible for recruitment into the RAMC until he gave in and let her join. She served throughout the war, sometimes applying her technique of a good slap to shell shock victims, and then afterwards in the Colonial Medical Service, before retiring to Chislehurst.

Holly was a woman of indomitable self-belief in the face of which most people gave way. She would frequently relate stories, in the thickly accented, fluent but idiosyncratic English which never left her, which always ended with unchallengeable certainty ... "and so they said, Holly, you were right and we were wrong". John and Mary had met her when she was "helping" at Celia's birth in Penang. Quite how much help she actually was, I'm not sure.

But her luxurious mansion flat on a hill in Chislehurst in South East London was quite unlike anything I had ever seen. Unlike most housing in Britain at the time, it had central heating, which Holly kept cranked up to blood heat. It was carpeted throughout, full of tapestries, statuettes and ornaments from her travels and work in South East Asia and South America, together with reminders of her Viennese childhood. In the 1960s, only 20 years or so after the end of World War 2, Zionism and support for Israel was unchallenged, and Holly was a keen Zionist. I avidly read her library of books about the Warsaw ghetto uprising and the movement towards the establishment of the state of Israel. She would never talk about what had happened to her family.

Quite what John and Mary were thinking when they entrusted UK parental duties for Celia and me to Holly isn't clear, but life with her in the winter holidays was certainly interesting. She was quite short and stooped, with a shock of white hair and a gimlet stare, partly a result of her extreme short-sightedness. She was a brilliant cook, who seldom bothered with recipes, and couldn't read them anyway. Hygiene was less important or visible to her; plates used often to arrive back for use with a large dollop of yesterday's meal, despite her early adoption of items like dishwashers and sink waste masticators ("Mr Rubbish Eater") which used frequently to grind to a halt on cutlery dropped down into it by mistake)

Her driving was lethally forceful. Nothing was ever her fault; after close encounters with other motorists, she would wind down her window and shout "Learn to drive!" while Celia and I attempted to recover our positions from whatever corner of the car we had been flung into. The car, incidentally, was a Hillman Minx convertible, probably now worth thousands if it had survived, and I derived major street cred from her visits to Bradfield in it. She was unable to park in anything less than 3 car lengths of space, which even in 1964 was hard to find in an urban shopping setting and meant that we would take hours over any car-borne expedition.

Her correspondence with John and Mary, and with mystified school authorities was conducted via a portable typewriter with several wonky keys. If you added in her short-sightedness and eccentric approach to English language and culture, her letters were ridiculously hard to decipher, and often required expensive phone calls or telegrams to sort out.

Life evolved as a succession of school terms, winter and Easter holidays with Holly and the glorious summers back home. There was one exception to this routine; John and Mary paid for us to fly out for one Christmas holiday (EI would only stump up for one return passage for each child per annum) during this time. This was a bittersweet experience: On the one hand it was wonderful to revisit the old Christmas routines of our childhood, but on the other the contrast between the cold grey of England and the hot primary colours of Malaysia, for only half the time of the summer holidays, was highly stressful.

During this time, I moved from age 13 to 17, and Celia from 11 to 15. I seemed to navigate these fragile years with less upset than Celia, who says now that she felt my eldest child status, and the role I had taken on as her protector, allowed her licence to rebel in the traditional teenager way. As a relatively elderly single woman of foreign extraction Holly had few contacts with children our age. I remember some excruciating sessions at the local church youth club, and one occasion when I danced with the daughter of one of her central European friends, who, despite this experience nevertheless went on to be a prominent Labour MP. Since Bradfield was determinedly male only and my opportunities for contact with the opposite sex there limited to joint choral performances of the Messiah with the local girls' public school, I was completely unused to dealing with girls by the time school ended. This may have been another factor in my inability to form lasting relationships.

My time at Bradfield encompassed the explosion of pop music in Britain and then around the world. It's hard to explain now the impact of this development. My parents' musical tastes included Russ Conway, Winifred Atwell and Burl Ives, and there wasn't such a thing as youth music. Towards the end of my time at Durlston (in 1963) The Beatles released Please Please Me, their debut album. Their first single from it, Love Me Do, had come out the previous October, to mild interest, but it was the second single, Please Please Me, which came out in January 1963 that launched them and the irreversible rise of pop music, made by young people for young people.

I remember hearing the single, and then John Lennon's hoarse voiced, shouted version of Twist and Shout, and knowing that things had changed for ever. Their effect on popular music and culture was seismic, and stunned the grownups, but also shattered the generational divide between future generations. John and Mary did not understand or like it. I could not imagine going to see Russ Conway with my parents, but in a reversal of roles, one of my great recent privileges has been to see Bruce Springsteen on Broadway with my son.

There were limited opportunities to hear this new music. The BBC sternly refused to play it and, in any case, we were not allowed radios at Bradfield until we moved from dormitories to studies. Into this gap fell the pirate radio stations. Exploiting a gap in the law which gave the BBC a broadcasting monopoly, they began broadcasting from small ships and redundant anti-aircraft gun platforms just outside UK territorial waters. They pumped out pop music 24 hours a day to the music starved youth of the swathes of the country which could receive the signal. My favourite station was Radio Caroline, broadcasting from just off Frinton-on Sea in Essex. Then, as now, Frinton was an ultra-respectable little community which did not even allow Fish and Chip shops, but for a few years it became the focus of British youth, which swarmed down to the seafront to engage in Frinton Flashing; switching your car headlights on and off in response to exhortations from the duty DJ on Caroline.

This was usually Johnnie Walker, who had the late-night slot, and played Percy Sledge's "These Arms of Mine" and "When a Man Loves a Woman " around extracts from letters from love struck fans. I was a member of his fan club, and that of Roger "Twiggy" Day- Your Thinner Record Spinner. Johnnie maintains a foothold in the airwaves to this day, with his "Sounds of the Seventies" show on Radio Two.

It was all too good to last. Harold Wilson's supposedly modern Labour Government passed legislation which filled the legislative gap in the Beeb's monopoly and sank the pirates. Caroline limped on, supplied from Holland but most of the DJs were recruited by the new land based pale imitation of the pirates; Radio One.

In 1967 tragedy struck with the dreadful deaths of Devi and Veloo. John was away from the estate. Technically, Veloo was not supposed to use John's car in such circumstances, but on this occasion he and Devi drove in it to the local village post office to withdraw money. On the way there he ran head on into a Mercedes taxi holding five people and all seven of them were killed.

I was told this news by Mary who was in England at the time and allowed to place a call to the Housemaster's study for me to take, but as far as I remember, neither she nor Celia, nor I were able to be together for mutual comfort. John and Mary never spoke to us about the aftermath of their death. I know that John devoted a lot of resources and energy to sorting out their estates and transferring them to Pany, their eldest son. All the children except Ravi were already living away from the estate: Pany was a medical orderly on another estate, and Santha and Vasantha had started their own families in Sungei Patani. Ravi had been due to fly to India the following day to begin pre-university studies but cancelled his journey for obvious reasons. There was no understanding at school of the extent of my loss. Murf, who was in any case an old school master type, and wouldn't have passed any exams in empathy, put a hand on my shoulder as I sobbed on the phone, but seemed genuinely mystified as to why I should be so upset.

As far as my friends were concerned, Devi and Veloo were just servants in a place far away of which they knew little and cared less. And even if they had understood, emotional expression was absolutely not acceptable. I felt more devastated and alienated than I ever had in the years I had been at school in England.

Celia, by contrast was treated very kindly; called out of a school assembly and told privately by the Headmistress but was as devastated as I was. Like me, she felt she had lost a mother.

My memories of our five-year sojourn with Holly are largely happy ones, and I continued to have a close and loving relationship with her until her death in 1987, visiting her for meals more or less monthly. These became increasingly unhygienic and inedible as her eyesight dwindled to absolutely nothing. The beginning of the end came when she had to stop driving. One of the very few regrets I allow myself to have, is that I hadn't kept sufficiently in touch with her to know when she became terminally ill and died. This happened quite quickly and was handled by her distant relative in the USA, who didn't alert me until after her death. Her funeral service, which John and Mary attended, and which was, also coincidentally, the last occasion I saw John, was a perfunctory affair handled by a bored rabbi from the Reformed tradition and was in no way an adequate tribute to an extraordinary woman.

Reflection: Looking back on our childhood, with its weird combination of boarding education in two countries, single annual contact visits with our parents, and unsuitable guardians, it's surprising that Celia and I survived even as well as we appear to have. Everything that happened to us was considered at the time to be completely normal in the middle-class circles in which we moved. As I have said elsewhere, we were lucky that all three of my boarding schools and four of Celia's (she was asked to leave one very posh girls' boarding school for destroying a nationwide study into the effectiveness of vitamins!) were largely free of the worst examples of the child abuse of which we are now aware, but the boarding school system itself is at least open to the charge of being itself abusive. At the same time, it is true to say that these circumstances also enabled early adoption of independent decision making by us.

CHAPTER 24

Endings

"It was 20 years ago today; Sgt Pepper taught the band to play". The opening words of the Beatles' new album ring out from the rather small speakers available at the Penang Swimming Club for about the fourth time in the last couple of hours. Roland is sitting on the terrace of the club looking out at the lights of Georgetown and the shipping anchored in Penang Roads. He's just heard the news that the estate which has been his true home all his life is to be sold and the family will be going "home" to the UK.

It's the annual party for the expat kids, and he has met the daughter of a major at the Gurkha Training Depot, also due to close soon. For both it is the last summer in Malaysia, but that is about all they have in common. He has no idea how to talk to girls, having met very few who aren't related to him, and anyway he is consumed with unhappiness about leaving Malaysia. They have a couple of uncomfortable dances- Sgt Pepper's isn't a very danceable record - before calling it quits. A couple of days later, they meet at the Passing out Parade for new Gurkhas, and things aren't any easier then. But Sgt Pepper's will always carry with it the memories of that evening and wondering what might have been, with her and if he could have stayed connected with Malaysia.

In July 1968 Celia and I flew out to Malaysia for our summer holiday, not knowing that it was going to be our last. Unbeknown to John, Eastern Industries had decided that the estate was to be broken up and sold in small bits to smallholders. The company had taken the view that synthetic rubber had made the natural product uncompetitive and was pulling out of the market.

1968 was high summer for the 60s. I was 17 and bought a copy of Sgt Pepper's Lonely-Hearts Club in a record shop in London while a Guards band marched past outside (a coincidence I think). I played it constantly. For the first and only time, Celia and I flew out separately, and my flight landed in Bangkok, with an overnight transit stop at what seemed an incredibly posh hotel before a connecting flight to Penang. My request for a wake-up call was ignored and I had extraordinarily little time to get myself to Don Muang airport. For the only time in my life, I was able to tell a Taxi driver to "step on it", and he complied enthusiastically. We made it and on board, like young males everywhere, I was bowled over by the gorgeous Thai flight attendant, the infatuation confirmed by her willingness to serve me a beer without batting a beautiful eyelid.

The early part of the summer proceeded as usual, unaffected by some rather unimpressive A level results on my part. About halfway through the holiday, John got the news that STP estate was being sold and he, along with the staff, would be redundant. I think he was not entirely shocked by the news, which came just after he had completed an extensive replanting programme which had stocked the estate with high yielding rubber. So desperate were EI to get rid of the estate that they were breaking it up into small chunks likely to appeal to smallholder rubber planters. This process was known as fragmentation and had been the fate of many of the large European owned plantations in recent years. It was a short-sighted commercial decision, rendered so by the Yom Kippur War three years later, which generated an oil boycott making synthetic rubber, which was made from oil, uncompetitive with the natural product. On the other hand, it extended opportunities for local smallholders to own productive rubber trees at a knock down price.

Things moved extremely fast after that. John was offered at least one other job, as a visiting agent (a kind of rubber estate inspector), but Mary insisted that she had had enough of their life in Malaysia and started to plan their return. Thanks to the taped interview in 2004, we can see how much of a sacrifice Mary had made in abandoning her hard-won social work qualification to go with her husband to Malaya. While the children were at home, she could at least convince herself that she had maternal responsibilities, even though Devi carried out most of these. But when the children went to the UK to school, that fig leaf went, and she had to fall back on her nursery school and the juvenile bench., honourable occupations themselves, but not the career she had desperately hoped for. I was making my University choices at the time, and in an act of complete lunacy, opted for the only two colleges offering Malay or South East Asian Studies. These were the School of Oriental and African Studies in London and the University of Hull in, well, Hull. In retrospect it's clear I was clinging on to my tattered and disrupted life in and love for Malaysia.

Our return to the UK meant that our staff also lost their jobs. Devi and Veloo were of course dead, and Pany, Santha and Vasantha were married and settled elsewhere. Ravi had entered higher education in India (he had decided to go after all, a couple of months following his parents' death) funded by Pany and money saved by Devi. John also helped with the purchase of a house for Ramu on Division 1, and he retired after their departure. The two gardeners also received payments. John's Chief Clerk took over management of the largest chunk of estate and moved into our house when John and Mary left.

The rest of the holiday passed in a blur of farewells and packing. When Celia and I left, we had a final goodbye with Ramu. In fact, I was to see him again two years later when I returned to Malaysia on a semi-authorised study tour, and attended his son, Krishnan's, wedding, but this was the real goodbye to a lovely man who had been a vital part of our life. The toast scraping, the cake mixture leaving, the helpless giggles with a tureen in each hand were all now over, and I was devastated.

I can't imagine what it must have been like for John, overseeing the destruction of his estate, and his life in Malaysia after 22 years. It was the end of a connection going back nearly 30 years, starting with the chaotic defeat in Singapore, terror and starvation in the jungles of Thailand, followed by a near civil war and a renewed life on a rubber estate. How had he thought it would end, I wonder? Compared with other end of empire experiences, it was reasonably civilised on all sides.

Mary too was sad, though it had been she who in insisted on drawing a curtain over their life in Malaysia. Too many years of contact with family via five-day-old aerogrammes, and even though life was very safe from the early 60s onwards, her fears from the days of the Emergency had never really gone away. These fears were never for her, they were for her family, from whom she was separated by her own decision to send us away to school. In later life, she went through further agonies as both her children travelled extensively overseas

Some years later she was asked to talk to the WI in the Somerset village they had settled in, about her years in Malaysia. This is what she said:

Malayan Memories- notes for a talk to Woolavington WI.
Northern Malay/Malaysia as it is now, where I spent over 20 years; for all but six months of this time, plus leave periods, on the same estate where our two children still feel their roots are, and where they spent their early years.
A land of paddy fields and rubber trees, tin mines and kampongs, jungle clad hills and red laterite roads....
My first impression of Malaya as the ship sailed into Penang roads was green, green and then more green, a piercing blue sky reflected in the calm sea, and the shores really were lined with palms, though mangrove swamps where the python lays (?) were also much in evidence and made the scene sinister as well as exotic.
I remember dark, smiling Malays in sarongs, more sober Chinese in varieties of clothes with more purposeful walks and Indian women with sari and the grace of classical beauty.
It is hard to remember the bad things, there was little evident poverty-the houses on stilts in the harbour teemed with life- no one seemed

hungry or miserable; clothing was kept to a minimum- everyone was occupied. We upstarts probably felt there were almost too many children, but they were so happy and the abundance of natural resources, vegetation, of fish in the sea- work on the estates or mines even two years after the end of the war meant that there was a purpose to life.

Up on the estate where we settled down to become part of the local community & to bring up our family the overwhelming feeling was one of joyous living despite the now continual guerrilla war waged by Communist led Chinese bandits and the fact that Malaya was a country of three main racial divisions- Malays, Chinese and Indians with their different religions and customs. Kedah was a state dominated by the Malays and Islam, but we never felt threatened as Christians & from the first, our church life was happy and fulfilling.

My first impression of the little ex garrison church on a hill in our nearest town where the harmonium was very temperamental(I played it often until rescued by a nurse from the hospital (a Chinese Malaysian) who banged out the hymns in true Salvation Army style), the fans ineffective but the congregation of Chinese, Indians and Europeans worshipped with great reverence and faith. I remember house meetings on isolated estates with our friends who put us to shame with their faith, and carol singing parties of young people going 50 miles in any direction.

I remember the coming of our Indian driver and wife who had decided that we were not managing as well as we might and later, our Indian cook. These three and their families became part of our family in a way no other people have done, and it was hard to reconcile ourselves when a few years before we left "Devi" and "Veloo" were killed in a car crash. We were however able to help their children become established and as things go full circle, now their youngest child at 40 is manager of a rubber estate and doing the same job he says, with the same principles as my husband did.

I could tell you stories of the emergency, of shooting and strikes, of the heartbreak of leaving one's children at home (ie UK) to be educated because the local schools did not take expatriates- of monsoon storms- attacks of malaria and dysentery, of injustices and high handed officialdom but these are not the things about Malaysia we easily remember. I know that time blunts the edges of all memories but when I ask my children what they remember, well they reply the happiness and the feeling of meeting people from different cultures and making lifelong friends of them (though they do remembers the partings at airports with their mother in dark glasses at the dead of night)- the parties we had in our bungalow of 30-40 people from the church, young people dancing and barbecuing and yes-communicating outside on the lawn while we adults put the world to rights inside. As we sailed out of Singapore harbour for the last time in 1968 I couldn't see the green or the paddi fields or the jungle clad slopes for my tears that we were leaving behind our friends and a land we loved which we might never see again.

And they never did.

PART THREE

CHAPTER 25

A New Life

It is May 1969 and Roland is in a top bunk in a Jerusalem youth hostel. He and Jaime have spent the day looking at newly "liberated" Dome of the Rock and Wailing Wall. Tomorrow, they will get the train back to Haifa, where he will board the ferry to Cyprus. At nearly 18, he is already a news junkie, and is listening to the World Service news on a little transistor radio.

Brian Barron, then the BBC's South East Asia correspondent, is broadcasting a report from Singapore about disturbances in Kuala Lumpur.

In the recent general election, the Alliance, a Malay dominated multi-racial coalition has lost its two thirds majority in parliament. This is important because that majority allows the Alliance to change the constitution at will. The main gainers are a multiracial party based in Penang called Gerakan Rakyat Malaysia (Malaysia People's Movement) and the DAP (Democratic Action Party), a largely Chinese and Indian oriented party.

Within a day of the election and fired up by ultra-religious and nationalistic Malay politicians, Malays from the areas of the city where they live-as a minority, and from Kampungs (villages) outside KL, riot in non-Malay areas, including the business district. The police (largely Malay) soon lose control and the army is brought in.

The first troops in are the Malaysia Rangers, largely recruiting from East Malaysia. They try their best to calm things down, but their relative even handedness does not go down well with the "ultras" and they are replaced by the Royal Malay Regiment, who allegedly support and encourage the Malay mayhem.

A state of emergency is declared., Tengku Abdul Rahman resigns as PM to be succeeded by Tun Abdul Razak at the head of a National Operations Council. The election results are declared void and measures introduced to consolidate Malay economic and political supremacy.

Shell shocked from my grief-stricken departure from my home, I stayed on at Bradfield for the winter term of 1968 to take Cambridge Entrance, and pretty much as I wanted, failed to get in. Murf wanted me to stay on for the rest of the year, partly to run B House as Head of House and partly to improve my A Level grades. This was unattractive for two reasons: I had no wish to try to contain the rising tide of rebellion making itself felt in Britain's public schools in the wake of the Summer of Love. And I failed to see why my parents should have to pay a further two terms' fees for the College to employ me on internal security duties. So, I finally left school in December 1968, with applications under way to the only two universities which offered South East Asian studies, and which seemed unworried by my less than brilliant A levels.

John and Mary arrived back in the UK for good in April 1969, after a round the world tour by ocean liner which had, remarkably enough, included a visit to two Rotary clubs in Japan and another one in Korea (He had been a Rotarian for some years, and had founded the SP Club branch).

Remarkable because of what happened at the end of the war. Until the atom bombing of Hiroshima and Nagasaki, the Japanese state was digging in for a long war of attrition following an Allied invasion of Japan. As we have seen, in Thailand, Allied officer POWs, including John, were being assembled in one camp, with a view either to being used as hostages or just for slaughter.

The destruction wrought by the atomic bombs convinced even the most diehard members of Hirohito's court that it would be necessary to surrender. But when the Emperor made an exceedingly rare radio broadcast to announce it, the word "surrender" was never mentioned. The closest Hirohito came, was to tell his people that "the war situation having developed not necessarily to Japan's advantage" the Japanese Army would stop fighting.

By the time the war ended, the US administration was becoming concerned at the disintegration of the KuoMinTang Chinese government in the face of Mao Tse Tung's People's Liberation.

They saw Japan as a potential counterweight to the threat posed by a communist China and the Soviet Union. Accordingly, and unlike in Germany, they looked to keep the Japanese state, including the Emperor, intact and in place. Thus, there was no Japanese equivalent to the reparations and compensation paid by the new German state to the survivors of its camps. John and every other POW received the grand sum of £76 and no apology. In 2000 they each received a further £10000 but that, sadly, was too late for him.

Despite this, John refused to hold a grudge against the Japanese people. In fact, in terms of day-to-day brutality, he regarded the Korean and Taiwanese colonial subjects used as guards as worse than the Japanese, and he wouldn't countenance the refusal of some of his colleagues to have anything to do with anything Japanese.

Like many who were caught up in the Malayan campaign disaster, he primarily, and in my view, correctly blamed Britain's own civilian and military leadership for what had happened to them. I am also convinced that the almost complete lack of post-traumatic stress support also contributed to his early death in 1987. Unlike Germany, Japan never fully accepted responsibility for its actions in instigating the war and its inhumane treatment of the civilians and military personnel it defeated.

On their return, John and Mary settled in Woolavington, the Somerset village where Mig had settled after the war. They quickly became central to the village's church and wider life. John became choir master at the church and joined the parish council.

Breaking the pattern of his fellow former expatriate colleagues, many of whom settled in warm climates such as Southern Spain, played golf and drank themselves to death, John retrained as a schoolteacher and then taught at Woolavington's primary school, while Mary taught at a local private school. Here, at last, she was able to resume a professional career, 20 years after having given one up to accompany John to Malaysia. After John retired, she continued to teach, while he happily looked after the house and the cooking.

John made an unusual primary school teacher. A middle-aged male in a largely female profession (he was the only male teacher at not only his school, but about half a dozen others in the area), he came with the life experience of a soldier and work and life overseas, added to which were a magnificent bass voice, choral experience and love of amateur dramatics. His lessons wove all these things into his teaching, as were his nearest and dearest; when visiting after a summer in upstate New York as a camp counsellor, I was roped in to talk about America and US holiday camps.

He rapidly won the hearts of students and teachers alike, and when on playground duty there were seldom fewer than three or four small children hanging off him. His kids were massively enthusiastic, and John loved the way they would hoist their arms in the air in order, he felt, to open wireless communications- his wartime speciality. If picked, only then would they devote any thought to the actual question. Usually they had not the faintest idea what the answer was.

To all intents and purposes, therefore, John led a peaceful, productive life. He joined the Far East Prisoners of War association, which agitated for a better deal for his fellow captives, but found the unforgiving approach adopted by their representatives did not sit well with him. He and Mary retained close links with our friends and colleagues in Malaysia, but quietly resisted invitations to return for visits.

He was part of a medical research study at Liverpool University, following POW survivors, but never talked about his experiences, except for occasional humorous anecdotes, and revealed little of his feelings about what had been done to him. Most of the material in this book has been obtained from documents and memorabilia he left behind, or from other family records. But in, the early 1970s, a few years into his second, teaching, career, John suddenly broke down, and could not continue to work. His recovery was slow but apparently successful, making full use of his Christian faith and the support of Mary and of Woolavington's vicar, a close friend. I remember going to visit him at a spiritual retreat he was attending as part of his recovery; I found him little changed from the gentle man I had always known.

Having ended his teaching career, John spent his remaining years in quiet retirement. His faith remained central to his life and accounted for another crisis a few years before he died. He had continued to lead a choir of all ages in the village church, and chaired the parish council. He worked hard to sustain the church with its shrinking congregation reflecting wider patterns of church non-attendance. In this he was aided and supported by a fellow ex colonial, from Kenya, who had also settled in the village.

The crisis was precipitated by the arrival in the early 1980s of a priest from an inner-city parish to look after the village church. It seems that the new incumbent wanted to change many things about his new parish., including the lack of engagement of a newish council estate, and the involvement of my father and another retiree with an ex colonial background.

The new priest scrapped the choir and much of the existing infrastructure of the local church. state, while establishing new services on the estate, which remained resolutely non-attended until eventually cancelled. I can remember talking to John about this. He was bewildered, since the choir, which had a membership of a dozen or so, usually included at least one or two people from the estate who he would take to and from the church for rehearsals and services.

The main issue was the way the new priest's behaviour had caused unhappiness and misery. But I think for John, the priest's assumption of a title to which he was not entitled was symptomatic of the man's disregard for the norms of good behaviour and order, which John would have craved above everything. And his upbringing would have made it difficult for him to express in words what he was feeling. Sadly, his letter to the man's boss, the bishop, focussed on this perhaps less important aspect of his behaviour.

Not surprisingly, John's grievances weren't addressed and his unhappiness was such that he and Mary moved from their Somerset village to another on the Somerset/Dorset borders, and from a small bungalow to an even smaller one. I can't now remember why they moved to this village, but one positive result was in John's faith. The new parish church was in the care of a charismatic priest called Tim Biles. Tim quickly endeared himself to John by taking him at face value and engaging him in frequent theological discussion.

Reflection: At this distance, John's row with the new vicar of Woolavington seems petty. But it upset John and Mary enough to decide to move away, and I think that was the case because said vicar had displayed such contempt for good manners and the feelings of his parishioners. One might have thought that this was nothing compared to what he had gone through in Thailand, but that experience had hugely weakened his ability to tolerate stress of any kind, with the results that followed.

EPILOGUE

After the Railway: An Afterword

October 1987: I am in a meeting, to which I have cycled, with a high-powered property developer and the Director of Housing at Tower Hamlets Council, about a development of his on the Thames at Wapping, which my housing association was about to acquire. The Developer is very keen to complete the deal, as am I. The Director of Housing's PA comes in and says "Mr Crooke, Mr Sigsworth from your office is here with an urgent message". I find out then that when they say in books "my blood ran cold"… it does. Don Sigsworth is our finance manager, a large, slow moving Yorkshireman with a broad Tyke accent and deliberate phrasing. I remember him being at the other end of a corridor and lumbering towards me. He blurts out "Roland, your father's died". Everything then becomes very still; I am finding it hard to stand and walk but go back into the office and announce "I'm sorry, I have to leave the meeting; my father's died". I will always remember the expression on the developer's face, not sadness, not sympathy, but irritation.

Don and another colleague, Abdul, have driven together to my meeting. Abdul drives me back to our office while, Don, heroically for a man of his proportions, rides my bike. From then on, things are a blur. I think Abdul drives me to my home, where I meet my uncle Pat, and together we drive down to Dorset. By this time, my parents' favourite vicar and his wife have arrived with food and practical help. My mother is very still and calm, as is her wont in a real crisis, mostly concerned at the burden she sees as falling on me and, when she ar-

rives shortly thereafter, Celia.

In 1985, after 12 years of work first at the Ministry of Defence and then in the social housing world, which I got into largely because their dress code permitted jeans, I became the Director of a small, very odd housing association, which, for utterly unfathomable reasons had properties in both Tower Hamlets and Maidenhead.

In that spring/summer of 1986, the Association recruited a new manager for its Maidenhead properties. My deputy Lynn and I interviewed a not very promising shortlist of candidates, including someone called Helen, at that time processing housing benefit claims at Reading Borough Council, with very neat handwriting but little apparent relevant experience.

Our Maidenhead office was a converted garage, with space at a premium. To interview candidates, Lynn sat at right angles to them on a chair, while I perched on a desk. Helen turned up in an elderly maroon Morris Minor car.

Helen was the owner of the neat handwriting and had applied the same organised approach to her application. Her lack of housing management experience was, she explained, not an issue since she could be trained. What counted was her ability to manage staff. This was certainly an issue since the small but motley staff team in the Maidenhead office included Harold, who had been in submarines during World War Two and who had been off sick for many years while fitting in a bit of caretaking on the side without bothering the Inland Revenue.

We arrived at the point in the interview when the applicant is asked if they have any questions, and it was at this point that Helen made a smash and grab raid on my heart. The normally expected response is "No, thanks, I think they've all been answered during the very thorough interview we have just completed". It is not, as one visibly drunk interviewee for a surveying post once said to me; "s'pose there'sh no point ashking about the colour of the car?". And it is extremely unusual for an applicant to extract from her file (labelled "Toynbee job") an A4 sheet with an exceptionally large number of superbly written questions on it and start going through them. Helen was good enough to concede that some questions had indeed been answered, but we were given a very thorough grilling on matters such as training opportunities and car loans.

At the end of it all, she strode out, and for all the wrong reasons we decided to appoint her. And to paraphrase Ms Bronte, reader, I married her - eventually.

Meanwhile, in Dorset, after the upset with the hostile vicar, John and Mary settled in happily to retired life in their new home on the border with Somerset. Mary joined the WI and John started a choir, again. Both were in demand with local clubs as speakers about Malaysia. They were visited frequently by Malaysian friends, local and expatriate.

I visited them regularly- monthly, and for Christmas, perhaps trying to make up for the years I hadn't been able to do so. I was sometimes alone, sometimes with a girlfriend if that coincided with the stage of the current brief relationship, or sometimes with my uncle Pat. Whatever the combination, I remember incredibly happy, comfortable, easy times with them. Now in my late thirties, and they in their sixties, our relationship seemed unencumbered by the normal parent/child baggage. They did not pretend to understand my career, relationships or for that matter musical choices, but seemed to have the wisdom to know that they couldn't alter them. John and I shared a sense of humour and we loved nothing more than reading aloud to each other choice passages from books like The Hitchhiker's Guide to the Galaxy. I was a keen runner, and John seemed to get a lot of pleasure out of timing my runs for me and providing water at prearranged rest stops. For no apparent reason, a welcome ritual developed between us, in which on arrival I would lift his glasses off his nose and reverse them before putting them back, a la Eric Morecambe. If I failed to do this, he would stand in front of me until I did.

Rajan and Ambika Menon, the last Chief Clerk on Sungei Toh Pawang, who had moved into our STP house and managed some of the fragmented estate, came to stay with John and Mary on a UK visit in July 1987. While John was driving to pick them up from Crewkerne railway station, another driver collided with the back of his car. Not John's fault at all, but the incident shocked him. I spoke to him shortly afterwards, and that shock was clear from his tone- possibly because of memories of Devi's and Veloo's accident. I thought about bringing forward my next visit, but didn't follow through, to my eternal regret. I have always wondered whether this accident triggered his death, coming as it did at an age (67) when the cumulative emotional and physical effects of his wartime captivity had already manifested themselves.

Because two weeks later, John was dead from what the death certificate said was a myocardial infarction, or heart attack to you and me. I was distraught with grief, but very conscious of the need to look after Mary, and Celia. At the thanksgiving service, I read the Hitchhiker's piece about the demise of the Frog Star Battle Machine at the hands of Marvin the paranoid Android. And because it would have made him smile too, I smiled in the hearse when the driver was trying discreetly to increase speed in a non-speedy way because we were late for our slot at the crematorium.

John's death was reported in the Malaysian plantation industry journal as a matter of great regret, and much was made of his being the driving force behind the establishment of Uplands school; the thing which had been intended to keep Celia and me safe, but which started the process of separating us from our home and the people we loved most. Waves of love and respect came from our friends in Malaysia.

John's death in July 1987 started a period of major mental fragility for me. That autumn, I was involved in a major row with the housing association's chair over her decision, without consulting me, to allow the vice-chair to move into a flat owned by the Association. In my view, this was a huge conflict of interest, and I reported it to our Regulator.

This rendered my position as Director pretty untenable, and when an offer of a post with the said Regulator came up, I took it, even though it was on a fixed term contract, and thus insecure, and was utterly different to anything I had ever done.

In early 1988 I started my new job. I was by this time involved in at least four substantial life events; a new relationship with Helen, the death of my father (and the earlier death of my much-loved guardian Holly), a career threatening job conflict and then starting a new, insecure job. In addition, I had taken on the guardianship of Celia's son, my 11-year-old nephew Luke, who, mirroring my own experience, was starting at a progressive boarding school in Surrey while his parents worked overseas.

In retrospect, it's not surprising that I fell apart emotionally at that point. I found the new job alien and frightening, and its insecure and short-term nature started to worry me immensely. I was trying also to support my mother, though from correspondence it's clear that she was trying to do the same for me. One silver lining to these dark clouds was Helen, who steadfastly supported me. Another, paradoxically, was my responsibility for Luke. Because I had been through his experience, I felt I understood him, although it was taxing to act as the occasional filter and interpreter of messages between the school and my sister about a boy with great intelligence and quirky personality. He used to spend most weekends with me. I would collect him from Waterloo station, and we would return to the house having picked up an entirely unsuitably violent video for him to watch, and a frothy romantic comedy for me. Those and a Chinese takeaway were standard features of our weekends together, which I loved.

My misery in the job was such by mid-1988 that I was close to resignation without any job to go to. An old friend came to the rescue with the offer of a job at the housing association he ran, and I practically bit his hand off.

In due course (in 1989), Helen moved out of the flat she had bought on her departure from her marital home and agreed to move in with me. This was the first time I had lived with anybody romantically and it proved to be an incredibly happy time, not at all terrifying as I had always thought such things would be. In June 1989 Helen became pregnant. This had not been a planned event- at least not with me. Helen took the view that she would love and look after our child with me preferably, but without me if not. It didn't take me long to realise that I very much wanted to be the father to our child.

So, on 3 Feb 1990, Thomas (Tom) John Elliott Crooke was born at Hackney's Homerton Hospital. His working title in utero, for no apparent reason, had been Norbert Dentressangle, after the exotically named French transport firm, but we were enormously proud to give him his grandfather's names. Three years later, after a move to Kent, Daisy Rachel Harriet Crooke (working title "Bobblehead", per TJEC) arrived

By the time Daisy was born in August 1993, I had not visited my home for over 20 years. In the summer of 1971, while at University, I had arranged a trip which was part study tour and part return to my home haunts. I had been privileged to be able to attend the wedding of Ramu's eldest son Krishnan, but also spent time in a Malay kampung (village) for the first time. I saw Santha and Vasantha, in their respective marital homes. It was poignant doing so; their lives had settled into contented domesticity and children were imminent, but they showed no less love and affection for us. Ravi (no longer Tambi), was in India doing an Agricultural course as part of his quest for a career something like John's. Pany, the eldest son, was now a medical assistant, working away from the area and so I didn't see him either.

In the intervening years we had been visited by both of Ravi's sisters, along with several of their relatives, an Ebenezer or two and at least one other graduate of Mary's nursery school. Tom grew used to a wider range of visitors than was the norm in East Kent among their friends.

By the early 90s Malaysia was on the brink of catapulting itself into first world status under the tri racial Alliance and its durable Prime Minister Mahathir Mohamed, a former GP from my home state of Kedah. Racial tensions still bubbled but below the surface, with an Islamist Malay political party which ran the east coast states of Kelantan and Terengganu snapping at his heels. Malay rights and privilege were entrenched in education and higher ed, with several Malaysian friends spending huge sums to send their children to Britain and other overseas destinations because they couldn't get access to Malaysian universities. There was strict government control of the media, but also the first stirrings of alternative voices in social media. Dissent was strictly controlled by the Internal Security Act, originally a piece of British colonial legislation, which the first post-colonial government had taken over and never repealed.

By 1991 I was Regional Director for Kent in the Housing Association I had joined in 1989.

In early 1993, I had joined Rotary, the international, but American based business networking and charitable organisation. John had helped to establish a branch of this august outfit in Sungei Patani in the 1960s and was proud of that, so I was equally proud to be asked to join and continue that tradition in his memory. The only mandatory requirement for membership was attendance at the weekly lunch, but it was also expected that after your family responsibilities, Rotary was your main spare time interest.

I found this, and the obligation to attend a weekly lunch meeting quite onerous; my work didn't often permit me to take the thick end of two hours out on a Friday for a bad lunch, when crises which had been brewing for the whole week tended to reach critical mass. But Rotary absolutely had my attention when it came to discussing 1993's Group Study Exchange (GSE) visit.

GSE was, and maybe still is, a Rotary annual programme which allows a small group of young businesspeople from one Rotary District to visit another in a different country for four weeks. Transport costs from District to District are met by Rotary HQ in Chicago, while all other hosting costs are met by the receiving District. The process is then reversed within the next twelve months. The visiting group is led by a Rotarian.

That year's GSE visit by the East Kent District was to be to Malaysia in November 1993. Daisy was due to arrive in July or August, making my taking part unthinkable, I thought, even if as a new Rotarian I was selected to lead the party- also an unlikely event.

Both these unthinkables turned out to be eminently thinkable. Helen was keen that I should go, despite the imminent arrival of a new baby and the extra burden this would put on her. She had come to understand the depth of my attachment to Malaysia, and we planned an extra two weeks after the GSE visit, during which she would fly out with the children to join me. I would then be able to show her round this country I called home. Encouraged, I attended an interview with the District Governor and Rotarian responsible for GSE. In the event, I was up against one other candidate, and it seems that my Malaysian experience outweighed my newness as a Rotarian, because I got the gig, as few Rotarians would put it.

Things moved fast after that. I managed to get leave to cover the four weeks of the tour and the two weeks of family visiting thereafter. The team I was to lead was picked, and Helen didn't blink when they proved to be four young women. We were to leave in early November, and by then had to be fully briefed on the country we were going to and have prepared a presentation to deliver to the Rotary Clubs we would be visiting. There were well over 20 of these, spread around the Malaysian peninsula, and when we finally got the programme it showed a packed series of visits and meetings. None of the team members had ever spent time in Malaysia or a similar tropical climate and they proceeded rather to wilt under the stresses of travel, climate, and the programme. They didn't really share my besotted feelings for the country, its people or even its cuisine, but I didn't let that spoil my wide experience of bits of the country I hadn't seen before and meeting new friends plus old family members. Our reception at the various clubs varied from sepulchral to riotous, particularly at the point in the meeting called brainstorming or networking, when most of the storming seemed to be done by Messrs Johnnie Walker and Jim Beam. Our presentation got mixed reviews, and sometimes wasn't even featured at all, as timings and arrangements generally seldom ran to plan.

Despite my pleas, Sungei Patani Rotary Club wasn't included in the itinerary, for reasons which eluded me, but Pany, working in the area and a former pupil of Mum's little nursery school Geeta, now a GP, were invited to an open house evening in KL. It was wonderful to see Pany after more than 20 years. He had Veloo's build, gait, and big ears, but he was altogether a more sensitive, wiser human being. We both burst into tears and hugged unrestrainedly, to the slight embarrassment of our host.

While touring the East Coast, the monsoon season arrived and my long-felt ambition to sing with a rock band had to be abandoned there half way through my spirited rendition of *"Hang on Sloopy"* ("Sloopy lives in a very bad part of town, and everybody, yeah, tries to put my Sloopy down") as a spectacular storm hit the hotel we were being entertained in.

Eventually, after what seemed like many more than four weeks, we ended up back in KL, where I said goodbye to the Rotary team at the airport departure gate before racing round to Arrivals to meet my own team.

It was wonderful to see them. Helen had flown for 13 hours with a three-year-old in the seat beside her and a three-month-old Daisy strapped to her. In those relatively relaxed days I was able to get into the hall after customs clearance and Tom wandered over to see me fully protected in a sweat top and jogging bottoms (in his three year old head it was still winter), which it took most of the next three weeks to get off him. Then Helen and Daisy appeared, apparently no worse for wear after the journey. Soon we were all packed into Pany's ridiculously small car with our luggage and deposited at Rajan Menon's house in Negeri Sembilan. The years had been good to John's former chief clerk and the house was comfortable. He had invited Ravi, Pany and their families over on the following day for an emotional re-union. Then we headed north.

The next two weeks were a whirlwind of renewed friendships and awed amazement at the changes of the last 20 years. Ravi was now a rubber estate manager, like John had been. He had generously loaned us his car and we used it to travel to parts of the country that were still familiar, and some that were new. We based ourselves for much of the time at the Lone Pine Hotel on the Penang coast, the very same hotel I had holidayed at with my parents and Celia all those years previously. Lone Pine had survived amid the soaring skyscraper resort hotels which now replaced most of the modest former colonial establishments on that strip of coast, and here, and indeed everywhere we went to eat or drink, three-month-old Daisy was whisked out of our hands on arrival and swept off to the kitchens or outside to be cooed over and shown round.

When we got back to Kedah, we re-established contact with Devi's family based there (Vasantha, Santha and their families), with the Ebenezers and other church people. Chelladurai (Chella), the oldest Ebenezer son, and his wife Helen took us to Langkawi island off the Kedah coast. This largely Malay populated island had been given duty free status, this having been removed from the largely Chinese island of Penang to its south and was being developed as a tourist resort. We crossed on a fast hydrofoil with incredibly violent kung fu movies playing, to Tom's fascinated amazement, had a lovely day before Chella remembered that the boat was leaving an hour earlier than he thought. For some reason, I was nominated to drive back to the ferry, a task I executed at top speed, reaching the port with literally seconds to spare. After that even a further diet of bloodthirsty karate kicks was relatively soothing.

Later in the trip we visited the old site of Uplands School on Penang Hill, as well as the school itself on its new site in Georgetown as a popular international school of the sort I could well have attended.... The familiar ache gnawed at my stomach as we approached the bottom station of the Penang Hill Railway. As I had done nearly 40 years before, we got off at the middle station and walked the mile or so to the school. Empty now and semi-derelict, it was still recognisable as the place I had spent the years from age 6 to age 9. I showed Helen, and Tom to the extent that he was interested, my old dorm, Celia's, the dining hall, and classrooms. I could almost see the groups of small children moving around the school and absently noted that it had been a gentle warm place to be - the aching feeling of loss at the bottom station was all about being deprived of my parents.

Contacts made in 1993 continued over the next few years, and we were visited by Vasantha, Chella, Helen and others. I conceived the utterly ridiculous idea of returning to Malaysia to work, and once again, Helen was up for the idea. In 1997 we hatched a plan to have a holiday in Malaysia, while I followed up the many opportunities which I naively felt were certain to materialise. By now, Tom, was 7 and much more receptive to the prospect of a visit. Daisy was 4 and of course hadn't registered her first trip, and both had been used to the steady trickle of Malaysian visitors in between times, so perhaps it would not be totally alien to them this time.

I spent a lot of time before we flew back to Malaysia researching possible work opportunities in the housing area with which I was familiar, to no great effect. This time, on arrival, we were met by what seemed like the whole of the Ebenezer clan at KL airport. Even more of them turned up for a rowdy banana leaf meal before escorting us to the old colonial, Moorish-style railway station to catch the overnight train to the North where the remaining element of the clan Ebenezer would be waiting for us. Our tickets had been bought locally for us by the Ebenezers, since it had proved impossible to do so in the UK, and they had plumped for 2nd class travel for us, rather than the 1st which I had requested. We were therefore accommodated in a multiberth compartment with shared lavatory in the next carriage.

We were all jet lagged and sleepless, and at one point Daisy asked to go to the loo on her own (four-year-olds do that).

The door opened by treading on a pressure pad and this was part of the attraction. Daisy brilliantly executed the manoeuvre and left the compartment before Helen could follow her. Helen then saw Daisy executing a handbrake right turn, heading towards the external carriage door, which could well open and deposit her out of the train into the warm tropical night. It felt like an eternity before Helen could get the door to open again and she was able to apprehend the fugitive inches from an uncertain fate.

After that, we tried to calm down, and get some sleep before we arrived to meet Helen and Chelladurai Ebenezer. Chella was senior medical officer for a chunk of rural Kedah and lived in a government compound which also housed his staff and their families. Tom and Daisy made firm friends with some of the children, despite sharing no languages, and played happily, just as I had done with children who could have been their grandparents 40 plus years before. Helen and Chella were childless and heaped love on my son and daughter, as I had known they would. With the instinct that only a childless adult can deploy, Chella gave Tom two things he desired more than life itself: A knock off Manchester United shirt and a toy rifle. His mother paled as these things were produced but kept quiet. Too soon it was time to leave, with friendships renewed, memories stored... But no job.

My miniscule chances of getting a job in Malaysia had been dealt a death blow by the financial crisis which hit Malaysia in 1997. Many of the economic gains accumulated over the last years were unravelled, and there were strains also at the top of the Malay element of the ruling coalition. PM Tun Mahathir sacked Anwar Ibrahim, his deputy and shortly afterwards Anwar was convicted on charges of sodomy (yes), and imprisoned. He spent most of the next 10 years in prison, while his wife Wan Azizah led the PKR, the new multiracial political party he had formed.

The prevailing dispensation, which gave Chinese and Indians a junior place at Malaysia's table, increasingly came under strain. Islamism had always had a hold over some Malays, and the Islamist party, PAS, had ruled the two East Coast states of Terengganu and Kelantan since Independence, but the use of the veil in its various versions was now almost universal for Malay women, whereas it had been rare to see it at all when I was young. Malay Nationalism fed on the economic crisis, which diluted somewhat the flow of benefits which had come the way of the "Bumiputras" (sons of the soil), but the overall dispensation seemed to hold good, albeit at the expense of democracy.

The next 20 years, spanning the end of the 20th century and start of the 21st saw great changes in all the characters in this story. Mahathir retired; one would have thought for good at the age of 78, were it not for his later return as the oldest Prime minister in the world. His successor, Tun Abdullah Seri Badawi, ushered in some years of relative liberalisation, but also increased unrest from the non - Malay peoples of Malaysia about Malay rights, electoral fraud, and just sheer naked corruption. There were major street protests in 2007, because of which Tan Sri Badawi was supplanted by Tan Sri Najib Razak, who became the 9th PM of the country. Najib came from Perak royal stock, the son of Tun Abdul Razak, the second PM. He seemed to promise a more liberal dispensation, with a few detainees under the ISA released and a promised review of the ISA itself. In practice, he seems to have spent most of his energies on truly industrial levels of corruption. In the elections of 2008 and 2013, the opposition, cross racial alliance made gains.

The rising power of China itself, and the meteoric success of the largely Chinese city state of Singapore reminded the Malay ultras that their room for manoeuvre was limited in the world of the early 2000s. My friends and family in Malaysia continued, for the most part, to prosper and live their lives unhindered. The younger generation were a different matter; they became increasingly moved by the levels of corruption in the ruling Malaysian elite and the worldwide "Spring" movements of the years after 2010. In this they were encouraged by the behaviour of Najib, whose greed and cupidity knew no bounds. He looted billions of dollars from the national coffers, ably assisted by his wife, Rosmah, who seems to have had a thing for handbags. As in, thousands of them.

The general Election of 2018 returned an opposition coalition called Pakatan Harapan (Alliance of Hope) to power, following a massive mobilisation of Malaysians at home and abroad. This was the first time that the opposition had come anywhere near power and there was hope of renewal and a non-racial democracy. The opposition's victory had been engineered in part by an operation mounted by young people in the Malaysian diaspora (many of whom, having been forced overseas for their higher education, had acquired an affection for the freedoms they found there) to bring home postal votes which had been disallowed through Government gerrymandering. Najib and his wife had been arrested and would soon be on trial.

In 2013, I had retired from paid work and taken up full time unpaid interfering in my local community. In early 2018, Helen was diagnosed with breast cancer, which she saw off with her typical determination, and less importantly, I had the latest in a series of joint replacements. Crises like these focus you on where and how you should be spending your remaining active years. I was conscious that it was 20 years since we had last visited Malaysia, and that 2020 would be the 75th anniversary of VJ Day, the Japanese surrender and John's release at the end of World War Two.

So, this seemed like a good, hopeful time to return home to Malaysia. But I was increasingly thinking in terms of committing our family's involvement with Malaysia to print. Mary, who had survived John by 20 years, was given a dementia diagnosis in 2007. Before her memory faded altogether, we had wanted to assemble her thoughts both written and not yet spoken. In 2004 her grandchildren Tom and Daisy had interviewed her about her life and recorded the conversation, which has shed much light on her role in this adventure. The transcript is attached as appendix 2.

I embarked on an account of John's war experiences which I entitled "An Ordinary Man", with invaluable help from the Bedfordshire County Archive and the Imperial War Museum and completed it in 2009. Tom and Daisy, who both take a more detached but still engaged view of Malaysia than I, said in late 2018 that they'd like to re-visit Malaysia, and Laura, one of Tom's university friends, now an academic specialising in British Social History, wanted to join a visit. It was she who encouraged me to write a wider account of John's story, his post war experiences, but importantly including the perspective of those living there through the end of colonialism.

And so it was that we arrived back in a much-changed KL just before Christmas 2018. A new airport, new monorail into the centre, huge skyscraper apartment blocks and malls and everywhere roaring, choking traffic. Our programme called for a few days in KL while we de-jetlagged and met up with Tom and Daisy (Life had overtaken Laura and sadly she had to drop out of the trip, while continuing to be engaged in this written work). Then we took the (new to us) train to Ipoh, our favourite city, before another train journey to Penang and a stay at Lone Pine in its new incarnation as a boutique hotel, and a final few days' vacation in Langkawi. An orthodox tourist itinerary, but this time I was also on the track of memories of John and Mary from Ravi, Geeta and the Ebenezers. Very sadly, both families had suffered loss since we had been there. Chelladurai had contracted Hepatitis B and died very quickly, leaving his lovely wife Helen widowed. Ravi's older brother Pany (some years earlier) and sister Santha (more recently) had both died under tragic circumstances, and in the case of Santha, there had been a rift between Ravi and her family which had still not healed.

Seventy-five years after the end of the second world war, Kuala Lumpur would have been unrecognisable to John, and almost to me after only 20 years' absence. It is a modern megalopolis whose outskirts sprawl almost all the way to the coast of the peninsula. Some efforts had been made to preserve bits of the colonial legacy; the railway station we had travelled from in 1997, lay rather sadly marooned in a sea of traffic, unused for long distance travel- that was now done by a huge transport hub, KL Sentral and a network of light and mono- rail tracks. The old Selangor State Secretariat, the hub of British power, and the Selangor Club (known as the "Dog") had been preserved around a central padang or field with the Anglican Cathedral on one side. If you made it through the traffic and squinted hard, it seemed as if nothing had changed- until you drew back and saw how these relics were surrounded by the hub of a modern city.

We quickly found that our best way to travel round was to use "Grab", the local variant of the Uber ride service. Malaysia has embraced all aspects of the new technology and media, and this App based service gave consistently reliable, clean transport and the chance for us to meet and talk to local people (the original vibrant mix of peoples in British Malaya having been further enriched by later arrivals, legal and otherwise, in a capital whose population was many times what it had been in the colonial era). My basic Malay was a help here, and we heard the stories of a range of people painting a picture of the opportunities and stresses of urban life in Malaysia in the 21st century.

But probably the most significant conversation I had was with Ravi. His career had moved from rubber estate management to that of oil palm plantations, and he was in the process of qualifying as an auditor in the industry. In 1993 he had replied to a letter I wrote to him warning of my return with the GSE trip. At that stage he had spent 16 years in rubber estate management, during which he had moved 12 times. This nomadic existence had continued in the 30 years after that, and in New Year 2019 when we saw him once more, he had just finished a stint in Sarawak, East Malaysia. We were invited to his house for dinner, which in Malaysia means some chit chat before going out to eat. With him were his wife Selvi, who we had first met in 1993, two sons, and his eldest son's wife. All were living in Ravi's large, ornate house, with the younger generation earning their living in various aspects of new technology.

The evening had got off to a slightly chaotic start when

we could get no response on arrival at his house. Eventually a slightly flustered Ravi emerged, clearly unprepared for our arranged arrival. Things got sorted out after a while, as they always do in Malaysia. We found ourselves talking about John. This was the first occasion on which I had ever really talked to Ravi about his relationship with John, and I was utterly moved by what he said.

"Roland, your father was an exceptionally fine man. Living in the same house, I got to know him very well, and I have modelled myself on him, tried to treat people in the same way he did, and conduct myself as he did. I knew his daily routine; He would get up early in the morning, as would my father, while it was still dark, put the dogs in the jeep and go on his morning tour of the estate. Then he would come back for his breakfast, as would my Dad. At this time, your Mum's school was starting, so cars would be arriving and leaving. Then my Dad would take him wherever he wanted to go, meetings or to the office- too hot for field work by then, unless he needed to deal with a problem. Back for lunch and a rest before going to the office to finish work for the day. Sometimes he would drive himself to the office so my Dad had time off. Every day the same, always polite and kind. He was the reason I decided to make my career in the plantation field."

I was overwhelmed by the detail and sincerity in what Ravi said. I knew that John and Mary had helped the family with cushioning funds on their departure and were deeply fond of all of them (Mary in her "interview" with Tom and Daisy says at one point *"they were supposed to be servants, but they were more than that; they were friends"*) but I had no idea of the depth to which those feelings were reciprocated. Similar thoughts are clear from Mangla's tribute, and Geeta, one of Mary's nursery school graduates spoke in similar terms.

And what of our Malaysian family and friends and the country itself? Malaysia, this imperial confection, both in terms of its inhabitants and its territory, has prospered economically at the cost of environmental degradation, a democratic deficit, and some racial tension. Its multiracial nature is the accidental result of various colonial imperatives to secure and process primary products like rubber and tin, and the fact that there has mostly been co-existence is a credit to its people. It has survived the colonial attentions of the Portuguese, Dutch, British, and most recently, briefly and violently, the Japanese, to end up now as a hugely successful city state in Singapore, and in Malaysia one of the more successful Asian economies. There has been rampant corruption in Malaysia, with well over 1 billion US dollars having been looted in one scandal alone. The promise of a Malaysian Spring in 2018 proved as illusory as it did elsewhere in the world. After the election of a new multiracial coalition ran aground on the rocks of communalism, power has reverted more strongly to the Malay populace in Malaysia, and the ruling party in Singapore has only very slightly loosened its grip. There has been little loosening of the restrictions on press and media freedoms in either Singapore or Malaysia.

And yet the increasingly assertive influence being exerted by China in the region and the world is making all the countries in the region look over their collective shoulder. China has always regarded the Chinese communities in the region as part of its diaspora, making regional governments think twice about policies towards those communities, economically vital as they are.

So, we come back full circle to that one day in the life of John Crooke, with which we opened this story. What can we say about that life? And what does it say about human contact between peoples within the experience of the end of Empire? We see that he lived his early life in relative privilege but the early death of his father in a pre-welfare state society imposed great strain on his family and forced him to take on early responsibilities as the head of the family. His sense of duty required him then to volunteer for the Army, and the terrible privations in the jungles he endured after defeat at Singapore were a consequence of that. His entirely voluntary return to the scene of his travail is at the same time incomprehensible and entirely understandable. He then led a professional and family life which touched people from many different worlds, his kindness and humility shining through the conflicts and difficulties of the time.

We have all been on a long journey over the arc of this story. John, Mary, Devi, Veloo, Pany, Ramu and Santha have all left us but Mangla is now proud grandmamma to Hunter Malachai, who appeared in 2019. His mum Debra, a music teacher, continues the choral tradition taught by "Mr Crooke", which would make him immensely proud.

Fittingly, perhaps, the black and white house which featured at the beginning of this story has gone back into the jungle from which it was carved, as have most of the elements of Sungei Toh Pawang Estate save the Hindu temple which we visited on our last trip, and the rubber factory. The Crooke family's second house now acts as a factory for birds' nests to use in the eponymous, and awfully expensive soup.

The empire which spawned them all is an historical footnote, and the region where the story played out has undergone massive change. John's story is of an ordinary man living through these times who faced extraordinary events and through immense courage and faith survived them to be loved and respected by many.

I want to give the last words to Ravi, who said the following about first Mary, in response to her heartfelt thoughts about his family in her interview:

"Only people who are genuine and sincere in their relationships with others have such feelings. Mrs Crooke(Mary) is one such person."

And about John:

"His was a difficult life from the age of 19 right until his untimely demise at a relatively young age of 67. But despite it all, it never showed up in his face, words nor in the way he lived his life. Such a man can best be described as an extraordinary man. Anything less would not be fair to him".

Selamat Jalan.   Berjaya Malaysia.

Fig 27: Gateposts marking entrance to the first house, now reclaimed by the jungle.

Roland Crooke
February 2020/July 2020

APPENDIX 1:

Ayo Gurkhali

Gurkhas have been an important part of John Crooke's life and that of his family. Their training depot had been moved to Sungei Patani, a few miles from Sungei Toh Pawang estate, after Indian Independence in 1947, when the Brigade was split between the Indian and British armies. The depot received the young men who had passed the extremely competitive selection process and turned them into soldiers. St Philip and St James' church. which we attended every Sunday evening, was next to the depot and our services took place to the background of young recruits running, marching or just chatting. The first school I attended after graduating from Mary's nursery school was an Army infants' school next to the parade ground, and lessons echoed to shouted drill instructions.

Gurkhas occupy a special place in the British Army and wider society. Nepal has never been part of the British Empire, and its citizens who chose to join the British Army did so without their families. Until recently they used to return to Nepal at the end of their service as honoured pensioners. Now they have been given the right to settle in the UK, as is right, but their service to Britain has always been given freely and voluntarily. This has been the case since they were first invited to do so at the end of a battle with the British Indian Army in the mid-19th C.

In the disaster of Singapore in 1941 the Gurkhas were the only part of the Indian Army contingent not to suffer wholesale desertions, and they suffered badly at the hands of the Japanese army. In the Malayan Emergency they constituted a high proportion of the Commonwealth forces and proved very skilled at jungle warfare, particularly Vasanthashes, which would be set for hours at a time, requiring soldiers to lie still and silent for all that time. They were fearless and lethal in close quarters combat, using their traditional kukri weapon- half knife, half machete. The knowledge that a Gurkha battalion was in the area was by 1955 a powerful incentive to defect for the sometimes demoralised MRLA fighters.

As local European dignitaries John's family would always be invited to the two parades which marked the end of the training for Gurkha recruits at the Depot. These were Beating the Retreat and the Passing out Parade.

Beating the Retreat is a traditional British Army ritual, commemorating the days when a regiment's standard was paraded in front of it at sunset so that the soldiers could see it before nightfall. The recruits would parade in their companies behind their British officers in white uniforms and the Depot band, including bagpipes (the Gurkhas had been taught to play the pipes by the Highlanders they had first fought against) as the sun went down.

The next morning, invited guests took their seats at dawn and the recruits would march out of the dawning sunrise, using the Light Infantry quick march they have always used as British troops, and march past a senior officer who had been invited to take the salute. This was the climax of their training and a huge moment for their British officers, this morning dressed in khaki drill shirts and enormous shorts. Legend had it that the shorts would be starched and ironed the previous evening by their batmen and placed standing in the corner of the officer's bedroom. He would then step into them the following morn.

As the British Army has contracted, the numbers of Gurkhas have diminished, until now there are only two infantry battalions, together with signals, logistics and engineers units. Still the passion and commitment of these soldiers burns as brightly as ever, and the competition to get into the British Army is as tough as ever. Today, recruit selection in Nepal is held jointly with the Singapore Police Force, whose Gurkha Contingent performs guard functions and acts as an emergency reserve in case of civil unrest. And as the British Army has struggled to recruit even the limited number of soldiers it now needs, a third battalion of Gurkhas has been raised.

It was our privilege as a family in 1996 to welcome three young Gurkha soldiers to our house for lunch when they were stationed as part of a reinforcement Company filling manpower gaps in a British regiment stationed near our home. Immaculately dressed, polite and cheerful, they made a fuss of our young children and gave Tom (aged 6) a present of a kukri, the curved knife/machete which is their symbol. He was well impressed, and for a long time there were carefully controlled viewings and handlings of the kukri, along the lines of their demonstrations.

They taught him their war-cry, too:

"Ayo Gurkhali!"- The Gurkhas are coming.

APPENDIX 2: INTERVIEW WITH GRANDMA, 23 OCT 2004

Dramatis Personae
Mary Crooke (nee Pagden, aged 83)
Daisy Crooke (aged 11)
Tom Crooke (aged 14)
Roland Crooke (aged 53)

Tom Crooke- gives date and title of event-An Interview with Grandma, and hands over to Daisy for some questions about Grandma's early memories and childhood.
Daisy: Whereabouts did you live when you were a little girl?
Mary: I lived in a place called Berkhamsted in Hertfordshire.
Daisy: Which is the earliest house you can remember?
Mary: I can remember a house that we only lived in for about a year and it was up at the top of Kings Road, a little terraced house, I think.
Daisy: Who lived with you? What was your family?
Mary: I lived with my father, my mother and my elder brother, Jack, who was three when I was born.
Daisy: Did you have any other brothers and sisters later on?
Mary: Later on, I had another brother and another sister.
Daisy; How did you get on with them
Mary: How did I get on with them? I think quite well. Just the same as any other family, we were a very close family, very fond of each other, but we quarrelled quite a bit.

Tom: About toys?

Mary: Yes, I suppose so....... I was supposed to be bossy, and the others didn't like me bossing them.... that was the thing, really.

Tom: I can almost imagine that, actually..... (laughter)

Daisy What sort of toys did you play with?

Mary: I can't really remember. I didn't like dolls. Mostly played out in the garden. We had a big garden- it was a big house which actually belonged to my rich aunt. It wasn't ours. We rented it and it had a lovely big garden. Whenever the weather was nice, we used to play out in it.

Tom: Did you play cricket or hide and seek or...?

Mary: Yes, Cricket and we didn't play football at all.

Tom: I don't suppose it was as popular then as it is now...

Mary: I don't think it was , no, in fact I'm sure it wasn't. And in my strata of society, or whatever you say, people thought that boys should play rugger, and I don't think they thought girls should play anything! (Giggles)

Tom: Yes, cooking or sewing, I suppose.

Mary: I played lacrosse. I was quite good at it. I was good at games, actually

Tom: That's (lacrosse) with the nets on the sticks.... Charlotte plays that.

Mary: A Canadian game- lovely game.

Tom: (prompts Daisy) school?

Daisy: What was the name of your primary school called?

Mary, I didn't have a primary school. I went to the same school from when I was 5 till I was nearly 17.

Tom: How big was the school?

Mary: 350, all girls. They went from 5 to 18. But I only stayed one year in the sixth form, because in those days you could get quite a cheapish education getting School Certificate which is a pre-runner to the GCSEs. You could stay on and do Higher Cert which was like A levels but my parents couldn't afford the fees any more because they had three other children to educate. So... and it was very difficult, because I wanted to go to university, but there were only two scholarships in the county for girls to get to any university and my parents again couldn't afford to let me stay on, get Higher, and Entry (to university)..

Daisy: Who were your friends, if you remember them?

Mary: My friends? Margaret Shattock, Margaret Long, Beatrice Chapman (giggles)

Tom: Wow, that's impressive- were these friends in sixth form or middle school...?

Mary; They'd come all the way up the school with me. Margaret Webster.....

Tom: Was it quite intimidating if you'd just started the school to have all the big girls as well as your age?

Mary: It might have been if we had all been in the same building, but in Berkhamsted there was a road called King's Road and one side was the senior school and on the other side was the junior part. So we only went in one part of the school from 5 to 10 juniors and then we went over but we didn't consciously ever have to change schools. Do you see what I mean? There were no, we didn't have any exams to pass or anything like that.

Our parents paid for us to go there, and I remember looking at the bill once, which my father told me I should never look at bills, they were for him, but I looked at the bill and for one term it was £5.

Tom: Gosh that must have been a lot of money ....

Mary: Yes, but I think it was cheap though because it was just a High School

Tom, Mmm, so not sort of Eton class then.

Daisy: I was going to ask when did you decide to change your name to Mary, instead of Lucy?

Mary: I didn't ever change it, I was always called Mary. I don't ever remember being called Lucy by my parents. They christened me Lucy Mary after my grandmother. My mother was very attached to her, but I was never unfortunately really like her. She was a really lovely person, so they called me Mary.

Daisy: What was the food like at your school and at home?

Mary: I never really had food at my school. I went at five... oh I should probably tell you: Before school I went to a little governess's. Do you know what a governess is?

A tutor, a spinster lady who took people in. From when I was 4 to when I was 5, my mother put me on the back of her bike and took me for a mile and a bit to the vicarage in a village where I had lessons with the vicar's children, where I had lessons for about a year, then I went to the big school, Berkhamsted High School. Is that alright? What was it you asked me?

Daisy: The food.

Mary: I didn't stay to lunch. Later on I did stay to lunch and it was alright. Yes, Yes. Except that they had fish, and I hate fish, as you know. Always have done. Always had fish on Fridays. Euuuuagh! And there's no way you cannot eat it. I mean you can't hide it.

Tom: Did you tend to eat a lot more red meat than you would do nowadays? More beef or lamb or pork....

Mary: We probably did have more meat. We only had fish once..... I can't remember us even having cauliflower cheese, but we might have done.

Tom: Nowadays there's all sorts of allegations over school dinners; pizza and chips, not very healthy. Would you say that your diet then was more healthier?

Mary: I don't think it was, actually. Perhaps it was in a way, but you see you had all these suet puddings and things like that which weren't very healthy, and I don't remember a lot of vegetables. And you had stew and I like my food.... and mince... and of course a big roast joint on Sunday, like a whole leg. Because there were 4 of us. And my father would sit at the top of the table...

Tom: and carve?

Mary: and carve it, yes. And my mother sat at the bottom. And we had a maid, to help in the house, and when we felt we were very rich we had two maids. We had a house up on Berkhamsted Common, which we went to when I was young. And then we had two maids and a gardener- I could rather do with one now, actually. My mother also seemed to do quite a lot in the house, and my father worked for the family firm, Cooper, McDougall and

Robertson, who made, and still do make sheep dip. My uncle - his father invented sheep dip in 1900 ish. So from that he got a baronetcy, which is why you have a relative called Lady Cooper.

Daisy: You said you had two maids; did they look after you or the house- do the cleaning, and things like that?

Mary: No, they did the cleaning. But when we were really prosperous, we had a nanny as well. That doesn't mean a grandmother nanny as you might call it today. She came to us when she was 16 from Falkirk in Scotland. She was terrified; she'd never been out of Falkirk in her life. There was no TV then for her so she could see how life was. She came down with no idea of what she was going to find. Anyway, she stayed with us for about 20 years, she married a chap from Berkhamsted. She went down to George Street, and had a house and had three children. Her husband had a little coal business. As far as I know, she's still there , but I lost touch with her in the last 2 or 3 years.

Daisy: Did you like her?

Mary: Loved her, yes.

Tom: And were you attached to all your house staff? Sorry, I don't want to call them that....

Mary: Yes, though the others they didn't stay as long. I think that as children, we regarded them more as friends than servants.

Tom: I don't suppose you were very upper class, more upper middle...

Mary: Yes, and they were a help to my mother. My father was never really very strong physically. He'd been in the colonial service in Kenya, and they invalided him out just before I was born, in fact. So he came back and took a job with my uncle's firm, but he never really enjoyed it. He was never fulfilled- he just wanted to be in the colonial civil service. He passed into the CCS from Keble College Oxford top.

Tom: Clever guy

Daisy: What did you decide to do after you left school?

Tom: What year was this when you left school?

Mary: Well, I was 17, one year after School Cert. 1938.

Tom: So just before the 2WW

Mary: Didn't know what to do, because I wanted to be a doctor but I had failed chemistry. Nobody would ever have taken a woman who couldn't pass all her exams, you know it was just no good at all.

Tom: Do you suppose they would have taken a man....

Mary: A chap, a boy, young man would have been taken out of his class and jolly well coached up until he got his exams.

Tom: So, a male dominated society....

Mary: Oh yes, for that sort of thing it was terrible and as I've said there were only one or two scholarships for girls.

Tom: Well, total credit to you for trying to keep on track and avoiding cooking, sewing etc.

Mary: Well, I wasn't any good at anything with my hands. Painting, sewing, anything like that.

Tom: Well I'm not particularly adept with that sort of thing either.

Mary: You mustn't say that love, you're very good.

Tom: Well that takes us up to 1938 and the end of school.

END OF SIDE

Tom: Side B This is about Grandma's war years and her time with the WAAF

Tom: OK Grandma, when you first heard that war had been declared, what were your first initial reactions?

Mary: I don't think you really knew what to think. I mean, no-one was particularly frightened, just a bit wondering where we go from here.

Tom: There had been a previous world war, world war 1, and the main enemy in that had also been Germany, so was there a feeling of confidence that Germany could be seen off again and you could be victorious again quite easily?

Mary: No, I don't think there was a feeling of confidence at all, except that possibly in the generation that had actually been through it and triumphed. But for my generation, no. We weren't frightened and had no thought that we wouldn't actually win. We were confident that it would be over at some point, just a matter of when.

Tom: Were you still living at home when war broke out?

Mary: Yes, I was planning to launch myself into the world.

Roland: What were you planning to do?

Mary: I'm not sure I knew what I would do. Because I had discovered that intellectually I would not be able to do the doctors' course and I was really looking around for something else to do. I think I was thinking in terms of hospital almoning, which now would be called medical social work, but in my day, I don't remember hearing about social workers. But I think that's what I was going towards.

Tom: When Britain started sending troops to France or its colonies, or wherever, did a lot of the men from Berkhamsted join up?

Mary: Not so much, because most of the men were already in the territorials. Your grandfather was one of those; he was in the territorials since he left school. Not so much the women, but it was the men you were asking about, wasn't it? And they, I mean I think some of them may have gone to the recruiting office but I'm not sure it happened that way because in a way we were already prepared for things to happen. There had been these territorials and I think it was over 16 or 17 you could join – and they had these camps, summer camps.

Tom: Did you feel compelled to join the war effort in any way?

Mary: I don't think so. I was very keen to do something, all my friends were. I had a friend who was a Quaker, and she was a conscientious objector. I think in a way we were a bit horrid to her, well not really horrid, but when we were talking about things we were going to do, we couldn't include her. Although we knew they did other things and everything. There were things they could do. That was my first encounter with Quakers; I didn't know anything about them before. But she was a lovely girl; I wonder what happened to her.

Roland: What was her name?

Mary: Beatrice Chapman.

Tom: What made you decide you'd like to be in the Women's Auxiliary Air Force, or WAAFs

Mary: Simply because everybody said "Mary, if you're going to join up you must join the WRNS. It's the ladies service", or my posh relatives said "We could find somebody who could give you an introduction to the FANYs", which is the First Aid Nursing Yeomanry.

Tom: Yes, Dad was telling me about that.

Roland: Yes, we were having a good old snigger about that.

Mary: I bet you were! Anyway, that was the only choice.

Tom: So how did you go about joining the WAAFs?

Mary: I put my best clothes on, went up to London. I was 17 I think. 18. I went to Adastral House, knocked at the door and said "I want to join the WAAFs". There were a couple of other girls there, but looking back now I realise they didn't get many applicants because they'd only just started in 1939.

Roland: So you were in at the beginning.

Mary. Yes. But do you know what they said to me? "Don't ring us, we'll ring you" so to speak. And I had to go home, but I made them write it down. The form I had to fill in said "what are you doing now?" And I had to say that I was teaching. Because I was helping at a Dame school.

Roland: Bobby Brewster's School!

Tom: Really! Wow! I remember those books, signed by the author.

Roland: Grandma's in them. Who are you, Miss......?

Mary: Can't remember, but I had all three sons of H E Todd (author) there.

Tom: What sort of qualities were they looking for if you wanted to join the WAAF because I suppose they covered a wide area. What did you need to get into the WAAFs?

Mary: Well, they wanted someone who was good at Maths, to become a plotter. I don't know why you needed maths, if you could see recognise your numbers....

Tom: And when did you start working for them properly and almost full time?

Mary: In Feb 1940 just before the Battle of Britain. Went for one-month recruitment depot at Uxbridge, where we learnt how to drill. My one memory of there is going to have a bath the first night in the barracks. There were no bath plugs, somebody had stolen all the plugs, so I had a bath by sticking a heel into the plug hole. I was terribly homesick. I cried. I'd never been away from home, except for a Guides' camp.

Tom: And during the Battle of Britain, when it was a stressful time with lots of young men being killed, did you find the job pretty taxing? Were there any times when you thought you couldn't carry on?

Mary: No, I don't think so. It was exhilarating, and when you're young, you don't think anything is going to happen to you. Happen to somebody else, maybe, but not to you. I always say that the war really did me good. It shook me out of my rut. It was quite scary too at times. Working underground, and you could hear the bombs and the place shook. That wasn't too good.

Tom: What was the main thing your job involved?

Mary: My basic task, well it altered as you grew more confident - first you were a runner and supplied everybody with what they needed...

Tom: Cups of tea?

Mary: That's right, and cups of tea for Churchill.....

Tom: We'll come back to that in a minute.

Mary: Then the earphones, then after a year you got an automatic promotion. You get a propeller on your sleeve and you're a Leading.... Anyway, I thought, I've had enough of this, so I put in for a commission, and I went up for an interview and I failed. I was furious.

Tom: I can't imagine you failing any test, Grandma.

Mary: Well I did, and I think it was because I was cheeky to the selection committee. They asked me what my father did! And I said, "I don't understand why you need to know what my father does", and they repeated it until I told them. So, we didn't part as particularly good friends and I found I hadn't passed. I was upset because I just wanted to get away. Six months later I applied again, and I then decided to be all smug and "I want to do something for the country". Luckily, they wanted codes and ciphers officers. They were doing a sort of trawl for them. It was around the time of Enigma, late 1940, 1941.

Tom: And was this around when you attempted to serve Winston Churchill tea?

Mary: Yes.

Tom: Would you like to give us an account?

Mary: Yes, I will. Picture the Ops Room floor, with everybody rushing round with their plotting sticks. There's a ping ping, and the duty corporal calls me over, and says the controller wants you, could you go up there please. I couldn't think what the controller wanted with me in the middle of the Battle of Britain.... and so I went all around and up the steps to this fishbowl place and a very young officer said "Tea for 6 please, and cheese rolls." And so, I looked all around to see who was there, and then I went down the steps and up 72 steps, except that we counted them, didn't we, and there weren't 72.

Roland: Yes, when we went back to Uxbridge and saw the ops room.....

Tom: Oh, I don't remember that...

Mary: I think you were there. I ordered the tea, had to make it myself. Made the cheese rolls, it was a huge tray, and you can imagine that the crockery was army, well air force. I staggered back downstairs again, then up a few stairs. I barely got into the ops place when this young man came to collect it from me. He said thank you, pushed me out and closed the door. Then I went back downstairs and stood with my hands behind my back waiting for somebody to call me to do something. There was a sort of pause, then you could hear the noise from the goldfish bowl, which I had thought was soundproofed. You could hear the laughter.

Then the bell went again, and the corporal said "They want to see you again". So up I trip, all unsuspecting, everybody's laughing, so I thought, "Oh goody!". The young man met me at the door but still didn't let me in very far. It seemed to me that everybody was looking at me and he said "you so and so", I can't remember what he said, but I don't think it was very bad language, because they were very gallant to us in those days. He said, "There's no tea in the pot."

Tom: Who was in the room?

Roland: Churchill was in the room!

Mary: Yes, Churchill, dying for his cup of tea!

Tom: Did you see him?

Mary: Yes, I did, he turned round at that point.

Daisy: Did he speak to you?

Mary: No, probably just as well, because he had an awful temper, and was probably quite cross. This young man was trying to make me feel not too bad, so down I go, but this time just with the tea.

Tom: And there's also an incident a bit later on involving Douglas Bader.

Mary: Oh, yes, I don't understand why his legs came to Uxbridge, but they did.

Roland: He had a flying accident before the war when he lost his legs, then he lost his false legs when he bailed out after he was shot down and left his legs behind. So he was in prison camp but legless.

Mary: I'm pretty sure that this was just one leg, I think they sent them separately. In separate drops. This was going to be dropped to him in France, so we were allowed to look.

Tom: Do you have any idea, because he was a renowned fighter pilot, how he flew his Spitfire or Hurricane with tin legs? Because he must have had to use the pedals.

Mary: No, I don't know how he did it, but long enough to get decorated! When he was promoted to Group Captain, he wouldn't have been allowed to fly, although they did still- no sorry, I don't know.....

Tom: I guess you remained in the WAAFS for the rest of the war?

Mary: No, I didn't. I went on with that job, then I got my commission, and I went to 1 OCTU at Loughborough, and then the 2nd OCTU at Headington near Cambridge where I learned the codes and ciphers trade.

Tom: So you were a code breaker?

Mary: Yes I suppose I was. And it was about the time of the Enigma though I didn't know about it then of course. But I used the TX machine. It was like a typewriter, but a bit bigger. I think it had letters on it, but it did something, so you didn't type the letter you saw.

Tom: The way it worked, it had dials which rotated after every keystroke made so that each letter you typed was completely random, and the only way you could make sense was by having a similar machine. Correct me if I'm wrong, but I think the way the Brits did it was by making an equivalent machine.

Mary: Well no, I don't know.

Tom: Was that the TX?

Roland: I think so. I think the TX was the machine that the Brits built to break Enigma once we had found the Enigma machine. Not that the Americans found it.

Tom (explaining): There's been a recent Hollywood movie about the crew of an American submarine who find an Enigma machine and destroy a large battleship and winning the war.

Mary: Well why are they allowed to do that?

Tom: I believe you had a fiancé at that time, who was in the Black Watch.

Mary: Yes, Derek. I was engaged in 1944.

Roland: We interrupted you. You got your commission. This would have been late 41 or 42. And then what happened?

Mary: I was posted to Uxbridge, where I remained for several years.

Tom: What was your job there?

Mary: I was.... After I got my commission, I stayed at Loughborough for a bit and learned how to take parades, and all sorts of things, I was posted as cipher officer to Oakington, which was in Cambridgeshire. It was a bomber station, and they had Stirlings, that's quite unusual, not many people know about Stirlings.

Tom: No, it's mostly Lancasters and Halifaxes.

Mary: I think it was the last station to have Stirlings.

Tom: Were they quite old or dated planes?

Mary: They proved to be a death trap. They tried to replace them with Lancasters as quickly as they could, but they couldn't. I mean it takes a long time to build a Lancaster. Your sort of cousin (Frances Slade) used to ferry them across- they were built in America and ferried across by women pilots, of whom she was one, across the Atlantic. Very brave.

Tom: But in the end they didn't use them?

Mary: Oh, they used them quite a bit when I was at Oakington.

Tom: But mainly in the first half of the war?

Mary: That's right, yes, they didn't have an exceptionally long life. Because they found them to have high casualty rates.

Tom: Did you do any cipher work leading up to D Day. Looking back on it, do you think anything you did might have been used at D Day?

Mary: Yes, because I was very stupid and fed up being a cipher officer, all I seemed to get were messages to somebody else about clothes. It was boring you see. I was stupid enough not to realise that this was all building up, that they were getting supplies ready for the second Front.

Tom: And when it happened, was there a great state of jubilation in the population?

Mary: I had left. I'd been pensioned off by that time I stopped being a member of the WAAF officially in early 1945, medically discharged, but I'd been at home for a year by then, so I didn't function as an officer after about the middle of 1944.

Tom: Do you think your time in the WAAF gave you more self-confidence?

Mary: Oh, yes, lots of my generation, despite all the tragedies, the war was a marvellous thing, especially for women. Because it gave us so much more... we had very responsible posts and in every walk of life. We became much more independent of men.

Tom: Yes, at the end of the first war as well, it resulted in women getting the vote. After the second world war, where did you see yourself going after it?

Mary: Well, I discovered that in 1944, the government would

be giving grants to people to do further education, after they'd been invalided out the forces. It was quite a good grant. I found this from my Aunt, whose husband had been an MP and so she knew a lot of the MPs and one of them got me onto the board of the RAF and I was given a grant to go to university.

Tom: What did you study?

Mary: I went to the London School of Economics and I studied Social Science. But they wouldn't give me a grant for a degree because they weren't certain about my health- just mean!

Tom: What health problems did you have.

Mary: I was discharged from the RAF with a slipped disc and spine. I was in a plaster jacket for 9 months. Oh well we got by. I got a certificate in social science after a two-day exam. Then I did nine months with the hospital almoners which was medical social work and got a certificate from the hospital almoners. I got a distinction and passed out top.

Tom: And what career were you lining up for yourself?

Mary: They had asked me to do I was going to do what your mum's doing.

Tom: Psychiatric nursing?

Mary: No, Psychiatric social work. But by that time, I had re-met your grandfather, who had come out of Japanese prison camp. He suggested that it might be a good idea if we got married.

Tom (giggles) Oh, just on the offhand?

Mary, Yes, just on the off hand, "oh and by the way I'm going out to Malaya in another year.".

Tom: Now we've reached Malaya, Daisy can take over and will ask you about life in Asia. So, here's Daisy., with the next phase of Grandma's life.

Daisy: About what year was it when you moved out there?

Mary: 19.....48. Your grandfather had been out there for a year. I went out to join him.

Daisy: How did you travel there?

Mary: Your great grandmother came down with me to Southampton. There were very few passenger ships working after the war, at the beginning of the after-war period, and I was booked on a Danish boat. They were the only people taking passengers then, to where I wanted to go. I was travelling in a ship which was destined for 40 passengers, and there were 70, so we had to double up. In single berth cabins we had two berths, and in two berth cabins there were four. We were mainly women travelling out to join our husbands who had gone out before.

Daisy: When you got there, what was your house like?

Mary: My house was a bungalow. Actually, all houses were called bungalows, but they weren't all bungalows, mainly houses. But ours was actually a bungalow (ie single storey), and luckily for us it was made of stone, and that stopped the bullets coming through (Tom and Mary giggle) but we did move to a wooden one when your father and aunt were born.

Daisy: Did it have stilts?

Mary: No, it was a bungalow, so it wouldn't have stilts. But later when your grandfather was promoted, so to speak, and he had a bigger salary and they moved him to a bigger house. Was it on stilts? No, I'm getting muddled, now.

Daisy: Did you work on a rubber plantation?

Mary, Yes, we worked on a rubber plantation. He was manager of it. I think it was 15000 acres. Towards the end of our time there, it got smaller. That was partly because they discovered iron ore on it and a Chinese, no Indian contractor started… bought some of the land and started mining on it.

Tom: Did you have an Emergency so to speak while you were out there?

Mary: My goodness, yes. The day I got on the boat; the first rubber planter in Malaya was killed by bandits. So that wasn't a very pleasant thought, was it? And so. But the casualties weren't as bad as they hoped, no, anticipated. We had to have barbed wire round the bungalows and the offices. I had to have a body-guard if I went anywhere, and your grandfather had two, one who was always by his side, even in the middle of the rubber plantations

Daisy: What was the food like, compared to here?

Mary: It was lovely, yes. Much nicer. A lot of the expatriates didn't like it. They found it exceedingly difficult to like it. Mind you, some of them didn't try extremely hard. It was like nothing they'd ever experienced

Tom: Sort of curries and things?

Mary: Yes. We had a cook and a house amah, and eventually we settled with a couple with four children, who lived in the servants' quarters at the back- all very feudal. Your father and Celia grew up with these children and they were great friends.

Roland: And these two have met them; Pathy, Santha, Vasantha and Ravi.

Daisy: What was the environment like around you, where you lived?

Mary: Well, we lived on the edge of the rubber plantation, so we were surrounded, really by rubber plantation. Sometimes when they cut the trees down to plant new ones, we had a lovely view, otherwise it was mostly trees. You could see the jungle.

Daisy: What did you work as when you were out there?

Mary: I started a school, a kindergarten for 4-7s, for any children who wished to come to learn English and basic reading and writing. Because the local Malaysians didn't start school until they were 6. These children weren't children of labourers, because they couldn't afford it, but they started work early. At one time I had 23 children of 9 different nationalities. I'd better tell you: I had English, Italian, Eurasian, Malay, Chinese, American, Dutch, Sikh, Indian.

Tom: While you were in Malaya, what was your daily routine: what was your daily life like?

Mary: Your grandfather got up, incredibly early, about half past four or five- as he got more senior, it got later, about half past six, but he was always an early riser. I lay abed a bit, but not too long, because I'm not that type. I got up, and did things in the garden, I think. There really wasn't anything I had to do, and that could be a bit difficult sometimes. I would be brought a cup of tea in bed if I was there, or when I was dressing, and then I'd go downstairs and do a bit of gentle gardening while the gardeners did all the hard work. Then I would go round the garden and then back into the house. Really it was a question of finding things to do. If you employ people to do things then it's not very fair to take it out of their hands, because that's their raison d'etre.

Tom: Yes, it is. So you didn't find it oppressive or boring, while you were out there...

Mary: No, but I was very unfulfilled. You know, I'd got this Social Science distinction, and I wasn't using it at all. I applied for some social work in Alor Star, the state capital, but if I'd got it I couldn't have lived at home.

Tom: So now we have kind of skipped if you like and we are now on to Grandma's life in Malaysia. Grandma has told us that although it was a refreshing change, she did feel quite unfulfilled and so I would like to ask if that was why she started the nursery school.

Mary: Well, partly that and partly by that time, after a lot of trouble, we had got two children (4 and 2) who needed occupation so I started a little nursery school for any children of that age for people who wanted their children to learn English The estate schools taught them in Malay or Tamil.

Tom: The kids you taught, did they know a lot of English already, none, or a bit?

Mary: A lot of them knew a bit.

Tom: What was the normal school day at your school?

Mary: At my little school? They arrived at 8.30 in the morning. They arrived at the school room, which was our living room the bottom floor of our bungalow. I know, a bungalow only has one floor, but it had two. Your grandfather would be back for his morning breakfast, having been out in the rubber fields for 2-3 hours.

Tom: What was the first lesson for the children?

Mary: Well, it wasn't quite as planned as that, so I couldn't tell you exactly....

We had a little assembly. It wasn't a Christian assembly because there were so many different religions, but we'd have a little song about how nice life was.

Tom That's really good.

Mary: All in English, and they soon learned it, because they wanted to speak English. They were all hard-working little things. One Chinese man, a friend of ours, I think he was called Ah Kong, brought his small son, he stood him in front of me, obviously expecting an entrance test, and this poor little child was only 3. Anyway, he recited Hickory Dickory Dock in Chinese English you see. It was absolutely sweet, and he was terrified, and I said he doesn't need to do that "I'd love to have you, my love"

Tom: Well, it sounds exactly the sort of school I'd like to go to. And so, when Celia and Roland were born, did you find you had less time to do the school or did you keep it going?.

Mary: Oh yes, yes, though they were already born when I started the school. Was that right?

Roland: Yes, and I went to it for a little bit but then I went to Uplands. Why don't you tell them about Uplands?

Mary: I don't know why you don't tell them about Uplands.....

Roland: Because they want to hear about it from you. Dad started Uplands, didn't he?

Mary: The children were 7 and 5, no 6 and 4; 7?

Roland: I was 6(when I went).

Mary (coughing/sneezing). Well, we decided they needed a proper education. At that time the local English-speaking schools didn't take expatriates. At any rate, you weren't supposed to, I don't know why not. It was that sort of society you see...So you two had to , the two of them had to go down to Penang and up Penang Hill, where they had started a school for planters and tin miners' children

Tom: Called Uplands?

Mary: Called Uplands. It wasn't just for English people, it was for anyone who wanted to send their children there, but of course it was expensive, so..... And we tried your father as a full boarder, and it nearly broke my heart, nearly broke his heart, I think.

Roland: I was a weekly boarder first, and that was getting a bit much for everybody, I think. You weren't allowed to come and get me until Saturday lunchtime, then we all had to get up very early on Monday morning and rendezvous in Bedong somewhere to be taken back to Penang...

Mary: No, we took you down to the ferry....

Roland: I think there was sometimes another family involved....

Mary: Oh yes.... the Prices,

Tom: So Roland went to school and Celia followed him. Was there still the bandits posing a problem?

Mary: Yes, well that's why they went.

Tom: Were these bandits just anarchists or did they have political motives?

Mary: The people who were instigating them or motivating them had political motives, yes. Well, the communists wanted to take over the whole of the Far East, really.

Tom: And did you feel particularly threatened at home?

Mary: I nearly always felt frightened, but I was quite pleased that your father told me, quite recently, I think, that he never felt in the least frightened or threatened. I don't know if that was true.

Roland: Oh, it was true. I just thought it was terribly good fun having armour plating round our bedroom, and guns to play with, real guns. The SCs, the Special Constables.

Mary: Well they shouldn't have been showing you.

Tom: Did they really give you guns to play with?

Roland: Oh yes, they showed us their guns..... M1 carbines Tom.

Tom, Wow, they were quite heavily armed...

Mary: You know more than I did about it all.

Roland: They were pretty incompetent, I remember; they used to go to sleep.

There was a shift that was supposed to guard the house at night. They had a little pile of sandbags round a tree, the first level down in the garden, and they used to snuggle down there and go to sleep, or in the garage. And the only time it came close to us was when they were tracking a CT, communist terrorist, through the estate. Do you remember that?

I remember going to see the place where they caught him, and there were bloodstains on the ground, but we never actually saw a CT did we?

Mary: No, but do you remember the time... your father used to take you on Sunday mornings round what he said were the safe places ... on a drive round the estate, to give you something to do, and you stopped at the office, which was, presumably, fairly safe, and I think it was one of the soldiers, from the Ox and Bucks Light Infantry came up and asked if you would like to see a bandit pack.. and you said yes, they would.

Roland: Because they were useless at packing.

Mary: Well it's essential that you know that that was all that was said.

Roland: It's worth explaining that there were two words for the people on the other side; CT or Bandits.

Mary: We always called them Bandits. So you got back into the jeep and followed the soldier to where the pack was. Then my husband, your father, said to Celia. "Get down Celia, and see the pack." And there was a wail from the back seat. Everybody else got down and walked towards this, but Celia had stayed in the jeep while the rest of you presumably were looking at this pack. "I don't want to. I'm frightened the bandit might come out of the pack!"

But nobody had ever explained to her what a bandit was, so it was something to be frightened of. You see you can sort of dismiss children for not really knowing what was going on

Tom: How long were you in Malaysia for?

Mary: 23 years. I wasn't, I was there for 21 years, your grandfather was there for 22.

Tom: So Celia and Roland went to school in England.

Mary: Yes, but first they went to school up Penang Hill, but we've done that. Yes, they went when Roland was 9 and Celia was 7 they went to England to school .

Tom: Did you notice things change at all when they went?

Mary: Yes, it was horrible.. ... No no, that's not true, but I missed them terribly. It was quite different for your grandfather, who was working all the time, but I couldn't get a job, so I had to make things up to do. But it was alright, no I'm not complaining. I've never felt quite the same. I've always had a guilt complex that I shouldn't have left them at home.

Tom: In your house or bungalow, how many people were there- how many staff did you have?

Mary: We had a cook called Ramu. And we had the house ayah who was Devi and she was married to the driver Veloo. They were more than servants, they were friends. They were real friends.

Tom: What year did John stop working on the plantation, or did he retire?

Mary: He didn't retire, he was made redundant because they sold the estate. The owners, who were Eastern Industries, were based in London, they were English and shareholders all mainly English.

Tom: And when he was made redundant did you stay in Malaysia or did you go straight home?

Mary: We decided that the firm was going to pay us to take all our belongings home. So we had 21 crates of stuff to take home, everything we owned, apart from the house we owned in England

Tom: Where did you settle?

Mary: Initially, we went to Somerset to your great grandmother's. She very kindly got out of her house so we could have somewhere to stay, bless her heart, so we made our way. We bought a bungalow opposite her house, in Chertsey Close.

TAPE STOPS

ACKNOWLEDGEMENTS

"From the Woodlands to the Jungle", by Martin Fryer, chronicles the war history of the 5th Beds and Herts.

Leslie Froggatt's Memoir, quoted in Out in the Midday Sun, The British in Malaya 1880-1960, by Margaret Shennan.

"Singapore Burning" by Colin Smith, a detailed account of the Singapore catastrophe

"Behind Bamboo" by Rohan Rivett, written shortly after the war, and mentions John.

"The Battle for Singapore", by Peter Thompson, written from an Australian point of view.

Imperial War Museum for the war diaries of Cpls Lello and Henderson, and John's MI9 debrief form which details his progress through the camps.

"The Bridges of the Thai Burma Railway", paper for the US Public Broadcast System
"The Thai- Burma Railway", by Rod Beattie, curator of the Thai Burma Railway Museum.

"Care for the Caring" by Geoffrey J Knapman, A history of the Medical Sickness, Annuity and Life Assurance Society.

"Captive Audiences, Captive Performers", by Sears Eldridge, Macalester College. Detailed account of the entertainment efforts made by and for POWs.

An account by Robert Hardie, a PoW doctor of his experiences in the camps.

ABOUT THE AUTHOR

Roland Crooke

Roland was brought up during the fifties and sixties in what became Malaysia and retains a strong affection for and interest in the country. He now lives near Wood-bridge in Suffolk and is looking forward to becoming a grandfather. To pass the time until then, he enjoys walking in Suffolk's beautiful forest, estuary and coastal land-scape.

Printed in Great Britain
by Amazon